GREEK ENCHIRIDION

A Concise Handbook of Grammar for Translation and Exegesis

by

William Graham MacDonald

HENDRICKSON
PUBLISHERS
PEABODY, MASSACHUSETTS 01961-3473

17 January 1986

6 89 Bookstore

The NT Greek text used in the illustrations is that of *Novum Testamentum Graece*, 26th edition, edited by Kurt Aland et al., copyright © 1979, Deutsche Bibelgesellschaft, Stuttgart. Used by permission.

Copyright ©1986 by Hendrickson Publishers, Inc.
P.O. Box 3473, Peabody, MA 01961-3473

Printed in the United States of America

ISBN 0-913573-18-3

74292

CONTENTS

HOW TO USE THE GREEK ENCHIRIDION   1

HOW TO USE THE GREEK ENCHIRIDION

This 'handbook' (ἐν + χείρ + ἴδιον—'in one's own hand') summarizes the fundamentals of Greek grammar and syntax. It is set up as a reference manual for anyone who has been introduced to Greek by an introductory textbook and now is ready to work at translation and exegesis.

Paradigms, principal parts of verbs, charts, systematic statements about usage, and the techniques of textual transcription are featured. Placed in one's hand—not his ear—the *Greek Enchiridion* will teach only when the one wanting to see the grammatical structures reaches for its help. This manual is designed to make it easy to look up material about which one is uncertain. In many ways this grammatical compilation reflects my own need to have before my eyes a compact summary of grammatical and exegetical supports. It is no shame to carry in one's hand what one does not use often enough to carry fully in one's head. This Enchiridion justifies itself on the same principle as that of a dictionary. It is meant to be consulted. (See the extensive Index of Key Terms and Paradigms.)

The *Greek Enchiridion* is designed for both deductive and inductive study. That is, following the presentation of each grammatical principle, illustrations in Greek texts are provided so that one can see and analyze the grammar (inductively), and not just hear it (deductively) in the stated principles.

For three cogent reasons, 99% of the time the illustrations provide only the Greek text and its biblical reference: (1) If translation is provided immediately following each line of Greek text, there exists the danger of forming a dependency relationship with it, thwarting the inductive value to be had in tracing out the meaning for oneself. All the while the safety net of the exact location of the translations in English Bibles is there should one really need to use them. (2) Inclusions of translations would have the disadvantage of increasing the book size by 40%, and even more disadvantageously, of separating grammatical captions by about twice the space, making it all the more difficult to see the entire configuration of a section at once. Miniaturization is the key to visualization; it produces a greater "depth of field" as photographers say. (3) The examples chosen employ easy vocabulary as far as possible.

Most people seem to be taught beginning Greek from the same grammar their own teacher studied. For those whose introductory studies were from J. Gresham Machen's *New Testament Greek for Beginners* the following components of this handbook will be new material: anarthrous constructions, the ablative, instrumental, and locative cases, the pluperfect tense, usage within tenses, the optative mood, and the grammar of conditions.

In the analysis of cases, the designations of both the Sanskritic eight- and the Germanic five-case systems have been given on opposite ends of the same line. One can designate cases by the appropriate terms with which he feels most comfortable.

Considerable attention has been given to *textual transcription*, since this process of making the text flow into its natural subordinations and parallelisms both requires syntactical understanding and further clarifies relationships in the process of detection.

This work has been influenced not a little by my Greek teachers of the mid-fifties: Clarence B. Hale, Merrill C. Tenney, A. Berkeley Mickelsen, and Gerald F. Hawthorne, and a decade later, Frank Stagg. To each of these men I owe special thanks and appreciation.

1
VERBS, INFINITIVES, PARTICIPLES

VERB FORMS

The verb of a Greek sentence must be respected as its most important word as well as its most complex form.

Verb-Form Families:

-μι Verbs: δίδωμι, τίθημι, ἀπόλλυμι
These are very old verbs; they have disappeared from modern Greek.

-ω Verbs: λύω, βλέπω, παιδεύω
This is the most common verb family in biblical Greek.

Clans within the Ω Verb Family:

-άω, -έω, and -όω Contract Verbs: ἀγαπάω, φιλέω, τυφλόω
The short vowels are contracted out so that the dictionary form φιλέω becomes φιλῶ in the present indicative.

-λω, -ρω Liquid Verbs (having a frictionless consonant—λ, ρ—capable of being prolonged like a vowel): ἀποστέλλω. Note change of the liquid verb in the future tense: ἀποστελῶ; αἴρω, fut. = ἀρῶ.

-νω Nasal Verbs (a variation within liquid verbs): μένω, fut. = μενῶ

VOICE

The form indicating voice tells what to expect as to the relationship of the verb to its subject.

ACTIVE VOICE:

The subject produces the action. The subject may be a noun, pronoun, or a proper noun, or be found in the person and number of the verb itself as seen in these examples respectively:

ἡ γὰρ αὔριον μεριμνήσει ἑαυτῆς (Matt. 6:34)

ἐκεῖνος [= ὁ παράκλητος] μαρτυρήσει περὶ ἐμοῦ (John 15:26)

ἀνέβη Πέτρος εἰς Ἰερουσαλήμ (Acts 11:2)

τί οὖν ἐροῦμεν πρὸς ταῦτα; (Rom. 8:31)

PASSIVE VOICE:

The subject is acted upon, or receives the action. The verb has a different ending from the active voice and this alerts us to the passive meaning:

Χριστὸς **κηρύσσεται** (1 Cor. 15:12)   **ἐδιδάχθητε** (2 Thess. 2:15)

The divine passive implies God to be the unspecified doer of the action.

κατὰ ἀποκάλυψιν **ἐγνωρίσθη** μοι τὸ μυστήριον (Eph. 3:3)

4

MIDDLE VOICE:

Found in Greek but not in English, the middle voice seems to be a hybrid of the active and passive voices. *With a reflexive force the subject produces and receives the action.* The middle voice is to verbs what the dative case is to nouns; it has an interest "to" or "for" the subject, involving the subject in the consequences of the action. Compare the Hebrew Hithpael conjugation.

The middle forms are the same as the passive voice except in the future, future perfect, and first and second aorist. The ambiguity of the middle or passive forms of the present and perfect must be resolved from the context.

Contrast of the *Active* and *Middle* Voices of the Same Verb:

πείθω: persuade, Matt. 27:20
ἀπέχω: receive ['have from'] Matt. 6:2
ἀποδίδωμι: pay ['give from'] Matt. 20:8
ἀπόλλυμι: destroy, Mark 1:24
φαίνω: shine, give light, John 5:35

πείθομαι: obey, believe ['persuade oneself'] Heb. 13: 17, 18
ἀπέχομαι: abstain ['keep oneself from'] 1 Thess. 4:3
ἀποδίδομαι: sell ['give for one's own profit'] Acts 5:8
ἀπόλλυμαι: commit suicide ['destroy oneself'] Mark 4:38
φαίνομαι: appear ['give light to oneself'] Matt. 2:7

REGULAR VERBS:

A regular verb has six principal parts formed from the same root.

	Present	Future	Aorist	Perfect-Active	Perfect-Middle	Passive
e.g.:	λύω	λύσω	ἔλυσα	λέλυκα	λέλυμαι	ἐλύθην

From these principal parts all the tenses of the verb can be constructed or recognized. For instance, the imperfect is built on the present stem, and the pluperfect is built on the perfect base.

IRREGULAR VERBS:

An irregular Greek verb may have more than one way to spell a particular principal part, or it shows in whatever principal parts it has that somewhere in its history different roots have come together to form one verb. For example, like English's "go, went, gone" (in which "went" originates from a different root) the Greek word φέρω illustrates its irregularity:

φέρω   οἴσω   ἤνεγκα   ἐνήνοχα   ἐνήνεγμαι   ἠνέχθην

(The first three are heterogeneous, and the last four are homogeneous.)

Defective Verbs: These lack the forms for one or more voices. Numerous verbs are defective: ἔρχομαι, ἀγωνίζομαι, σεβάζομαι, δέχομαι.

Deponent Verbs: These verbs are defective in the active voice *but have an active meaning, although they are middle or passive in form:* ἔρχομαι, μάχομαι, ἐπίσταμαι.

Equative Verbs: Linking a noun with another noun or modifier, an equative verb (like εἰμί or γίνομαι): (1) does not take an object; (2) is not used passively.

Nominal Clauses: Sometimes the key non-verbal words of a clause or sentence are placed together without writing the implied verb to be, which the translator could easily supply.

καὶ ἡ ἐλπὶς ἡμῶν βεβαία ὑπὲρ ὑμῶν . . . (2 Cor. 1:7)
πιστεύετέ μοι ὅτι ἐγὼ ἐν τῷ πατρὶ καὶ ὁ πατὴρ ἐν ἐμοί (John 14:11)

KINDS OF ACTION

Kind of action is the major consideration in Greek tenses. In English the time of the action [past, present, future] is primary. But in Greek a tense denotes *how* the action happens in terms of its being linear, punctiliar, completed, or undefined, and it also indicates the *time* of the action in the indicative mood. Other moods determine the time from the context for translational purposes.

Simple action: Aorist tense

English has no aorist tense with which to compare it. The Greek aorist simply predicates action without indication of initiation or termination, completeness or incompleteness. This simplicity is sometimes described as being punctiliar, as seeing the action as a whole:

πραγματεύσασθε ἐν ᾧ ἔρχομαι (Luke 19:13—"Trade [the assets] until I come")

Symbol: a large circle   ◯

Note: The fallacy of thinking of the aorist as being a point in time (rather than a circle) can be seen in the following example:

τεσσεράκοντα καὶ ἓξ ἔτεσιν οἰκοδομήθη ὁ ναός (John 2:20)

Linear action: Imperfect and Present; sometimes the Future tense.

1. Continuous, progressive action:

τὸ φῶς ἐν τῇ σκοτίᾳ **φαίνει** (John 1:5)

Symbol: ———————

2. Repeated action in a series, i.e., iterative:

χήρα δὲ ἦν ἐν τῇ πόλει ἐκείνῃ καὶ **ἤρχετο** πρὸς αὐτόν (Luke 18:3)

Symbol: · · · · · · · · · ·

Punctiliar action: Context may indicate an Aorist, Present, or Future to be squeezed down to a temporal point:

Εἰσῆλθεν δὲ σατανᾶς εἰς Ἰούδαν (Luke 22:3)
ὁ ἀκούων εἰπάτω **ἔρχου**. καὶ ὁ διψῶν **ἐρχέσθω** (Rev. 22:17)
ἐλεύσομαι δὲ ταχέως πρὸς ὑμᾶς ἐὰν ὁ κύριος θελήσῃ (1 Cor. 4:19)

Symbol: ●

Completed action: Perfect and Pluperfect tenses; the action is culminated and endures as accomplished:

τὸν δρόμον **τετέλεκα**, τὴν πίστιν **τετήρηκα** (2 Tim. 4:7)
καὶ σκοτία ἤδη **ἐγεγόνει** καὶ οὔπω **ἐληλύθει** πρὸς αὐτοὺς ὁ Ἰησοῦς (John 6:17)

Symbol: ●———————

AORIST TENSE

STRUCTURE OF THE AORIST INDICATIVE

First Aorist:

act.:   augment + pres. stem + σα (3s=σε) + secondary endings: ἔ λυ σα α
mid.:   augment + pres. stem + σα (2s=σω) + secondary endings: ἐ λυ σά μην
pass.: augment + pres. stem + θη + sec. act. ends. ν, ς, -, μεν, τε, σαν: ἐ λύ θη ν

Second Aorist:

act.:   aug. + aor. stem + {var. vowel + sec. act. ends.:   {ἔ λιπ ον
                              {same as impf. after stem   {(ex. not from λύω but λείπω

mid.:   aug. + aor. stem + {var. vowel + sec. mid. ends.:   ἐ λιπ ό μην
                              {same as impf. after stem

pass.: aug. + aor. stem + η + sec. act. ends. ν, σ, -, μεν, τε, σαν: ἐ λίπ η ν

TRANSLATIONAL OPTIONS OF THE INDICATIVE MOOD INTO ENGLISH:

Since the aorist tense simply denotes occurrence without reference to initiation, progress, completion, or any such thing, it is usually translated from the indicative mood into English by a past tense. (The other moods will not be bound to show this past aspect of the aorist indicative.)

Active: ἔλυσε—he loosed;   ἔλιπε—he lacked
Middle: ἐλύσατο—he loosed himself;   ἐλίπετο—he fell short of himself
Passive: ἐλύθη—he was loosed;   ἐλίπη—he was in need

USES OF THE AORIST TENSE:

1. *Pure Aorist:* The action is characteristically viewed as a whole:

   The action may have endured over a period of time seen as a whole:

   [Ἡρῴδης] **ἐφοβήθη** τὸν ὄχλον, ὅτι ὡς προφήτην αὐτὸν [Ἰωάννης] εἶχον (Matt. 14:5)

   The action may have comprised telescoped events seen as a whole:

   ὁ θεὸς **λαλήσας** τοῖς πατράσιν ἐν τοῖς προφήταις ἐπ᾽ ἐσχάτου τῶν ἡμερῶν τούτων **ἐλάλησεν** ἡμῖν ἐν υἱῷ (Heb. 1:1–2)

   The whole action may have taken only an instant:

   ἐπαύσατο λαλῶν (Luke 5:4)

   Action not yet accomplished may be viewed as a whole:

   ἆρον τὸ σὸν καὶ ὕπαγε (Matt. 20:14)

2. *Literary Aorist:* A writer of a letter writes with the temporal perspective of his reader after the letter arrives.

   Ταῦτα **ἔγραψα** ὑμῖν περὶ τῶν πλανώντων ὑμᾶς (1 John 2:26)

3. *Periphrastic Aorist Construction:* This is a construction rather than a use and occurs only once in the NT—Luke 23:19 (Robertson, *GGNTLHR*, p. 375).

10

Paradigms of the Aorist Indicative Active

First Aorist: λύω

Active	Middle	Passive
ἔλυσα	ἐλυσάμην	ἐλύθην
ἔλυσας	ἐλύσω	ἐλύθης
ἔλυσε	ἐλύσατο	ἐλύθη
ἐλύσαμεν	ἐλυσάμεθα	ἐλύθημεν
ἐλύσατε	ἐλύσασθε	ἐλύθητε
ἔλυσαν	ἐλύσαντο	ἐλύθησαν

Second Aorist: λείπω

Active	Middle	Passive
ἔλιπον	ἐλιπόμην	ἐλίπην
ἔλιπες	ἐλίπου	ἐλίπης
ἔλιπε	ἐλίπετο	ἐλίπη
ἐλίπομεν	ἐλιπόμεθα	ἐλίπημεν
ἐλίπετε	ἐλίπεσθε	ἐλίπητε
ἔλιπον	ἐλίποντο	ἐλίπησαν

Liquid-Nasal Aorist: φαίνω

Active	Middle	Passive
ἔφηνα	ἐφηνάμην	ἐφάνην
ἔφηνας	ἐφήνω	ἐφάνης
ἔφηνε	ἐφήνατο	ἐφάνη
ἐφήναμεν	ἐφηνάμεθα	ἐφάνημεν
ἐφήνατε	ἐφήνασθε	ἐφάνητε
ἔφηναν	ἐφήναντο	ἐφάνησαν

The third letter of the active and middle is often α as it is in the passive.

More Paradigms of the First Aorist: Active Voice (λύω)

Subjunctive	Optative	Imperative	Infinitive	Participle	
λύσω	λύσαιμι			λύσας	nom. s.m.
λύσῃς	λύσαις	λῦσον		λύσασα	nom. s.f.
λύσῃ	λύσαι	λυσάτω		λῦσαν	nom. s.n.
λύσωμεν	λύσαιμεν				
λύσητε	λύσαιτε	λύσατε			
λύσωσι	λύσαιεν	λυ{σάντων / σάτωσαν}	λῦσαι		

First Aorist: Middle Voice

Subjunctive	Optative	Imperative	Infinitive	Participle	
λύσωμαι	λυσαίμην			λυσάμενος	nom. s.m.
λύσῃ	λύσαιο	λῦσαι		λυσαμένη	nom. s.f.
λύσηται	λύσαιτο	λυσάσθω		λυσάμενον	nom. s.n.
λυσώμεθα	λυσαίμεθα				
λύσησθε	λύσαισθε	λύσασθε			
λύσωνται	λύσαιντο	λυσά{σθων / σθωσαν}	λύσασθαι		

Additional Paradigms of the Second Aorist (λείπω): Active Voice

Subjunctive	Optative	Imperative	Infinitive	Participle	
λίπω	λίποιμι			λιπών	nom. s.m.
λίπῃς	λίποις	λίπε		λιποῦσα	nom. s.f.
λίπῃ	λίποι	λιπέτω		λιπόν	nom. s.n.
λίπωμεν	λίποιμεν				
λίπητε	λίποιτε	λίπετε			
λίπωσι	λίποιεν	λιπ{όντων / έτωσαν	λιπεῖν		

Second Aorist: Middle Voice

λίπωμαι	λιποίμην			λιπόμενος	nom. s.m.
λίπῃ	λίποιο	λιποῦ		λιπομένη	nom. s.f.
λίπηται	λίποιτο	λιπέσθω		λιπόμενον	nom. s.n.
λιπόμεθα	λιποίμεθα				
λίπησθε	λίποισθε	λίπεσθε			
λίπωνται	λίποιντο	λιπέ{σθων / σθωσαν	λιπέσθαι		

14

Additional Paradigms of the *First* Aorist: Passive Voice

Subjunctive	Optative	Imperative	Infinitive	Participle	
λυθῶ	λυθείην			λυθείς	nom. s.m.
λυθῇς	λυθείης	λύθητι		λυθεῖσα	nom. s.f.
λυθῇ	λυθείη	λυθήτω		λυθέν	nom. s.n.
λυθῶμεν	λυθείημεν				
λυθῆτε	λυθείητε	λύθητε			
λυθῶσι	λυθείησαν	λυ{θέντων / θήτωσαν}	λυθῆναι		

Additional Paradigms of the *Second* Aorist: Passive Voice

Subjunctive		Imperative	Infinitive	Participle	
λιπῶ				λιπείς	nom. s.m.
λιπῇς		λίπηθι		λιπεῖσα	nom. s.f.
λιπῇ		λιπήτω		λιπέν	nom. s.n.
λιπῶμεν					
λιπῆτε		λίπητε			
λιπῶσι		λιπ{έντων / ήτωσαν}	λιπῆναι		

Paradigms of the μ Conjugation (δίδωμι)

SECOND AORIST

	Indicative	Subjunctive	Imperative	Infinitive	Participle	
A	ἔδωκα	δῶ			δούς	nom. s.m.
C	ἔδωκας	δῷς	δός		δοῦσα	nom. s.f.
T	ἔδωκε	δῷ	δότω		δόν	nom. s.n.
I	ἐδώκαμεν	δῶμεν				
V	ἐδώκατε	δῶτε	δότε			
E	ἔδωκαν	δῶσι	δό{ντων / τωσαν	δοῦναι		
M	ἐδόμην	δῶμαι			δόμενος	nom. s.m.
I	ἔδου	δῷ	δοῦ		δομένη	nom. s.f.
D	ἔδοτο	δῶται	δόσθω		δόμενον	nom. s.n.
D	ἐδόμεθα	δώμεθα				
L	ἔδοσθε	δῶσθε	δόσθε			
E	ἔδοντο	δῶνται	δό{σθων / σθωσαν	δόσθαι		

Paradigms of the μ Conjugation: [Second] Aorist Passive

Indicative	Subjunctive	Imperative	Infinitive	Participle	
ἐδόθην	δοθῶ			δοθείς	nom. s.m.
ἐδόθης	δοθῇς	δόθητι		δοθεῖσα	nom. s.f.
ἐδόθη	δοθῇ	δοθήτω		δοθέν	nom. s.n.
ἐδόθημεν	δοθῶμεν				
ἐδόθητε	δοθῆτε	δόθητε			
ἐδόθησαν	δοθῶσι	δοθ{έντων / ήτωσαν}	δοθῆναι		

Paradigms of Liquid-Nasal Aorist Passive in the Oblique Moods (φαίνω)

Subjunctive	Imperative	Infinitive	Participle	
φανῶ			φανείς	nom. s.m.
φανῇς	φάνηθι		φανεῖσα	nom. s.f.
φανῇ	φανήτω		φανέν	nom. s.n.
φανῶμεν				
φανῆτε	φάνητε			
φανῶσι	φαν{έντων / ήτωσαν}	φανῆναι		

Paradigms of the Liquid-Nasal Aorist Oblique Moods

ACTIVE VOICE: φαίνω

Subjunctive	Imperative	Infinitive	Participle		
φήνω	φῆνον		φήνας	nom.	s.m.
φήνῃς	φηνάτω		φήνασα	nom.	s.f.
φήνῃ			φῆναν	nom.	s.n.
φήνωμεν					
φήνητε	φήνατε				
φήνωσι	φηνάντων / {άτωσαν}	φῆναι			

MIDDLE VOICE: φαίνω

Subjunctive	Imperative	Infinitive	Participle		
φήνωμαι			φηνάμενος	nom.	s.m.
φήνῃ	φῆναι		φηναμένη	nom.	s.f.
φήνηται	φηνάσθω		φηνάμενον	nom.	s.n.
φηνώμεθα					
φήνησθε	φήνασθε				
φήνωνται	φηνάσθων / {άσθωσαν}	φῆνασθαι			

VERB ENDING PATTERNS (Exclusive of Variable Vowels)

PRIMARY ENDINGS (Ω verbs)

Present	—Ind., Subjn.
Future	—Ind.
Perfect	—Ind., Subjn.
Aorist (1&2)	—Subjn.

Active

1	(ω)	—		μεν
2	(εις)	ς		τε
3	(ει)	—		σι, ν

Middle / Passive

1		μαι		μεθα
2	(η)	[σαι]		σθε
3		ται		νται

SECONDARY ENDINGS (Ω verbs)

Imperfect	—Ind.
Aorist (1&2)	—Ind.
Pluperfect	—Ind.

Active

1	(ον)	ν	μεν
2	(ες)	ς	τε
3	(ε)	—	ν, σαν

Middle / Passive

1	μην	μεθα
2	[σο]	σθε
3	το	ντο

IMPERATIVE (Ω verbs)

	Pres. Act.	Pres. Mid.	Aor. 1&2 Act.	Aor. 1&2 Mid.	Aor. 1&2 Pass.
2	(ε) τε	ου σθε	(ον, ε) τε	(αι, ου) σθε	(τι, θι) τε
3	το {ντων / τωσαν}	σθω {σθων / σθωσαν}	τω {ντων / τωσαν}	σθω {σθων / σθωσαν}	τω {ντων / τωσαν}

PRESENT TENSE

Structure: present stem + variable vowel (if any) + primary endings: λύ ω
dictionary   o or ε
form less   (before consonants)
ending

Active	1s = [ω]		1p = μεν
	2s = [ει]ς		2p = τε
	3s = [ει]		3p = σι
Passive	1s = μαι		1p = μεθα
	2s = -[σαι]		2p = σθε
	3s = ται		3p = νται

TRANSLATIONAL OPTIONS OF THE INDICATIVE MOOD INTO ENGLISH:

Active: λύει
(regular)   he looses
(progressive)   he is loosing
(emphatic)   he does loose
(iterative)   he keeps loosing
(historical)   he loosed
(futuristic)   he will loose

Middle: λύεται
(regular)   he looses himself
(progressive)   he is loosing himself
(emphatic)   he does loose himself
(iterative)   he keeps loosing himself
(historical)   he loosed himself
(futuristic)   he will loose himself

Passive:
(regular)   he is loosed
(progressive)   he is being loosed
(iterative)   he keeps being loosed
(historical)   he was loosed
(futuristic)   he will be loosed

USES OF THE PRESENT TENSE:

1. *Continuous Present:* The action endures without cessation:

ὁ κόσμος οὐ **γινώσκει** ἡμᾶς (1 John 3:1)

2. *Iterative Present:* Continual action under the right conditions is predicated. This may also be called the *Proverbial Present:*

ἕκαστος δὲ **πειράζεται** ὑπὸ τῆς ἰδίας ἐπιθυμίας (James 1:14)

3. *Historical Present:* A narrative passage relates with the excitement of the present what actually transpired in antecedent time:

ἔρχεται ὁ Φίλιππος καὶ **λέγει** τῷ Ἀνδρέᾳ (John 12:22)

4. *Futuristic Present:* A future act is so certain in the writer's thought that it is contemplated by him as if it were going on at the time of speaking:

ἴδε **ἄγω** ὑμῖν αὐτὸν ἔξω, . . . ἐξῆλθεν οὖν ὁ Ἰησοῦς ἔξω (John 19:4–5)

5. *Immediate Present:* The action continues momentarily:

Αἰνέα, **ἰᾶταί** σε Ἰησοῦς . . . καὶ εὐθέως ἀνέστη (Acts 9:34)

6. *Periphrastic Present Construction:* present of εἰμί + present participle

εὑρήκαμεν τὸν Μεσσίαν, ὅ **ἐστιν** μεθερμηνευόμενον χριστός (John 1:41)

20

Paradigms of the Present Tense

ACTIVE VOICE: λύω

	Indicative	Subjunctive	Optative	Imperative	Infinitive
1s	λύ ω	λύ ω	λύ οι μι		
2s	λύ εις	λύ ῃς	λύ οι ς	λῦ ε	
3s	λύ ει	λύ ῃ	λύ οι	λυ έ τω	
1p	λύ ο μεν	λύ ω μεν	λύ οι μεν		
2p	λύ ε τε	λύ η τε	λύ οι τε	λύ ε τε	
3p	λύ ουσι	λύ ω σι	λύ οι εν	λυ {ό ντων / έ τωσαν}	λύ ειν
					to loose
	I loose	I should loose	I ought to loose	2s loose	
		I may loose	I would loose	3s cause him to loose	
		I might loose		let [=make] him loose s.o. or s.t.	
		1p let us loose s.o. or s.t.		2p [all of you] loose	
				3p make them loose s.o. or s.t.	
				cause them to loose	

PARTICIPLE: λύων, λύουσα, λύον, etc. 'loosing' (full paradigm, p. 61)

MIDDLE AND PASSIVE VOICE OF THE PRESENT TENSE: λύω

Indicative	Subjunctive	Optative	Imperative	Infinitive
λύ ο μαι	λύ ω μαι	λυ οί μην		
λύ η	λύ η	λύ οι ο	λύ ου	
λύ ε ται	λύ η ται	λύ οι το	λυ έ σθω	
λυ ό μεθα	λυ ώ μεθα	λυ οί μεθα		
λύ ε σθε	λύ η σθε	λύ οι σθε	λύ ε σθε	
λύ ο νται	λύ ω νται	λύ οι ντο	λυ έ {σθων / σθωσαν	λύ ε σθαι

Indicative
I am loosing myself;
I am being loosed;

Subjunctive
I might* loose myself;
(Pres. subjn. is rare in NT)
1p Let us loose ourselves.
* may, should

Optative
I would loose myself;
(Pres. opt. is rare in NT)

Imperative
2s loose yourself; be loose
2p loose youselves; be loose
3s let/make him loose himself
3p cause them to loose themselves

Infinitive
to loose oneself
to be loose

PARTICIPLES: full paradigm, p. 62

More Paradigms of the Present Tense—Contract Verbs:

Active Voice of the *Contract Verbs*: πλανάω, λαλέω

Indicative	Subjunctive	Imperative	Infinitive	Participle	
πλανῶ	πλανῶ			πλανῶν	nom. s.m.
πλανᾷς	πλανᾷς	πλάνα		πλανῶσα	nom. s.f.
πλανᾷ	πλανᾷ	πλανάτω		πλανῶν	nom. s.n.
πλανῶμεν	πλανῶμεν				
πλανᾶτε	πλανᾶτε	πλανᾶτε			
πλανῶσι	πλανῶσι	πλαν{όντων / άτωσαν}	πλανᾶν		
λαλῶ	λαλῶ			λαλῶν	nom. s.m.
λαλεῖς	λαλῇς	λάλει		λαλοῦσα	nom. s.f.
λαλεῖ	λαλῇ	λαλείτω		λαλοῦν	nom. s.n.
λαλοῦμεν	λαλῶμεν				
λαλεῖτε	λαλῆτε	λαλεῖτε			
λαλοῦσι	λαλῶσι	λαλ{ούντων / είτωσαν}	λαλεῖν		

Present Tense of an Omicron Contract Verb in the Active Voice: πληρόω

Indicative	Subjunctive	Imperative	Infinitive	Participle	
πληρῶ	πληρῶ			πληρῶν	nom. s.m.
πληροῖς	πληροῖς	πλήρου		πληροῦσα	nom. s.f.
πληροῖ	πληροῖ	πληρούτω		πληροῦν	nom. s.n.
πληροῦμεν	πληρῶμεν				
πληροῦτε	πληρῶτε	πληροῦτε			
πληροῦσι	πληρῶσι	πληρ{οῦντων / ούτωσαν}	πληροῦν		

Present Tense of a μι Verb in the Active Voice: δίδωμι

Indicative	Subjunctive	Imperative	Infinitive	Participle	
δίδωμι	διδῶ			διδούς	nom. s.m.
δίδως	διδῷς	δίδου		διδοῦσα	nom. s.f.
δίδωσι	διδῷ	διδότω		διδόν	nom. s.n.
δίδομεν	διδῶμεν				
δίδοτε	διδῶτε	δίδοτε			
διδόασι	διδῶσι	διδ{όντων / ότωσαν}	διδόναι		

Present Tense of Alpha Contract Verb Middle or Passive Voice: πλανάω

Indicative	Subjunctive	Imperative	Infinitive	Participle		
πλανῶμαι	Same			πλανώμενος	nom.	s.m.
πλανᾷ	as Indicative	πλανῶ		πλανωμένη	nom.	s.f.
πλανᾶται		πλανάσθω		πλανώμενον	nom.	s.n.
πλανώμεθα						
πλανᾶσθε		πλανᾶσθε				
πλανῶνται		πλαν{άσθων / άσθωσαν}	πλανᾶσθαι			

Present Tense of Epsilon Contract Verb Middle or Passive Voice: λαλέω

Indicative	Subjunctive	Imperative	Infinitive	Participle		
λαλοῦμαι	λαλῶμαι			λαλούμενος	nom.	s.m.
λαλῇ	λαλῇ	λαλοῦ		λαλουμένη	nom.	s.f.
λαλεῖται	λαλῆται	λαλείσθω		λαλούμενον	nom.	s.n.
λαλούμεθα	λαλώμεθα					
λαλεῖσθε	λαλῆσθε	λαλεῖσθε				
λαλοῦνται	λαλῶνται	λαλ{είσθων / είσθωσαν}	λαλεῖσθαι			

Present Tense of Omicron Contract Verb Middle or Passive Voice: πληρόω

Indicative	Subjunctive	Imperative	Infinitive	Participle	
πληροῦμαι	πληρῶμαι			πληρούμενος	nom. s.m.
πληροῖ	πληροῖ	πληροῦ		πληρουμένη	nom. s.f.
πληροῦται	πληρῶται	πληροῦσθω		πληρούμενον	nom. s.n.
πληρούμεθα	πληρώμεθα				
πληροῦσθε	πληρῶσθε	πληροῦσθε			
πληροῦνται	πληρῶνται	πληρ{ούσθων / ούσθωσαν	πληροῦσθαι		

Present Tense of a μι Verb Middle or Passive Voice: δίδωμι

Indicative	Subjunctive	Imperaive	Infinitive	Participle	
δίδομαι	διδῶμαι			διδόμενος	nom. s.m.
δίδοσαι	διδῷ	δίδοσο		διδομένη	nom. s.f.
δίδοται	διδῶται	διδόσθω		διδόμενον	nom. s.n.
διδόμεθα	διδώμεθα				
δίδοσθε	διδῶσθε	δίδοσθε			
δίδονται	διδῶνται	διδό{σθων / σωσαν	δίδοσθαι		

IMPERFECT TENSE

STRUCTURE: augment + present stem + any variable vowels + secondary endings: ἔ λυ ον
ε   dictionary   o or ε   act. = ν, ς, -,
form less   (before conson..nts)   μεν, τε, ν
ending   pass. = μην, [ου], το,
μεθα, σθε, ντο

TRANSLATIONAL OPTIONS OF THE INDICATIVE MOOD INTO ENGLISH:

Active: ἔλυε

he was loosing
he kept [on] loosing
he used to loose
he loosed and loosed and loosed

Middle: ἐλύετο

he was loosing himself
he kept loosing himself
he used to loose himself

Passive: ἐλύετο

he was being loosed
he kept being loosed

USES OF THE IMPERFECT TENSE:

1. *Continuous Imperfect:* The action continues in the past to a less remote past—often right up to the present:

   ἡμεῖς δὲ **ἠλπίζομεν** ὅτι αὐτός ἐστιν . . . (Luke 24:21)

2. *Iterative Imperfect:* The iterative imperfect is *continual* (i.e., repeated) in the past as contrasted with continuous:

   καθ᾽ ἡμέραν ἐν τῷ ἱερῷ **ἐκαθεζόμην** διδάσκων (Matt. 26:55)

3. *Inceptive Imperfect:* Continued action is begun in the past:

[εὐθὺς] ἐλύθη ὁ δεσμὸς τῆς γλώσσης αὐτοῦ καὶ ἐλάλει ὀρθῶς (Mark 7:35)

4. *Inferential Imperfect:* A second class conditional sentence translates the imperfect in the apodosis by "could," or "would" as most appropriate, and not by the ordinary translational lingo:

εἶπεν αὐτοῖς ὁ Ἰησοῦς· εἰ ὁ θεὸς πατὴρ ὑμῶν ἦν, **ἠγαπᾶτε ἂν ἐμέ** (John 8:42)

5. *Periphrastic Imperfect Construction:* Imperfect of εἰμί + present participle. This use expresses continued action in the past.

Καὶ **ἦν** ὁ λαὸς **προσδοκῶν** τὸν Ζαχαρίαν (Luke 1:21)

Complete Paradigms of the Imperfect Tense
(The imperfect tense occurs only in the Indicative Mood.)

		Active Voice		*Middle or Passive Voice*	
1s	ἔ λυ ο ν	1p	ἐ λύ ο μεν	ἐ λυ ό μην	ἐ λυ ό μεθα
2s	ἔ λυ ε ς	2p	ἐ λύ ε τε	ἐ λύ ου	ἐ λύ ε σθε
3s	ἔ λυ ε	3p	ἔ λυ ο ν	ἐ λύ ε το	ἐ λύ ο ντο

I was loosing

I was loosing myself [or]
I was being loosed

28

The Imperfect of Contract Verbs

Structure: aug. + pres. stem + lengthened vowel or diphthong + secondary endings

Imperfect Active			Imperfect Middle or Passive		
ἐπλάνων	ἐλάλουν	ἐπλήρουν	ἐπλανώμην	ἐλαλούμην	ἐπληρούμην
ἐπλάνας	ἐλάλεις	ἐπλήρους	ἐπλανῶ	ἐλαλοῦ	ἐπληροῦ
ἐπλάνα	ἐλάλει	ἐπλήρου	ἐπλανᾶτο	ἐλαλεῖτο	ἐπληροῦτο
ἐπλανῶμεν	ἐλαλοῦμεν	ἐπληροῦμεν	ἐπλανώμεθα	ἐλαλούμεθα	ἐπληρούμεθα
ἐπλανᾶτε	ἐλαλεῖτε	ἐπληροῦτε	ἐπλανᾶσθε	ἐλαλεῖσθε	ἐπληροῦσθε
ἐπλάνων	ἐλάλουν	ἐπλήρουν	ἐπλανῶντο	ἐλαλοῦντο	ἐπληροῦντο

The Imperfect of μι Verbs

Structure: aug. + pres. stem (ending in a vowel usu. short) + secondary endings

Imperfect Active		Imperfect Middle or Passive	
ἐδίδουν	ἐτίθην	ἐδιδόμην	ἐτιθέμην
ἐδίδους	ἐτίθεις	ἐδίδοσο	ἐτίθεσο
ἐδίδου	ἐτίθει	ἐδίδοτο	ἐτίθετο
ἐδίδομεν	ἐτίθεμεν	ἐδιδόμεθα	ἐτιθέμεθα
ἐδίδοτε	ἐτίθετε	ἐδίδοσθε	ἐτίθεσθε
ἐδίδοσαν	ἐτίθεσαν	ἐδίδοντο	ἐτίθεντο

Verbal Contraction Chart

final stem vowels:	α	ε	o
endings: ε =	α	ει	ου
η =	α	η	ω
o =	ω	ου	ου
ω =	ω	ω	ω
ει =	ᾳ, α	ει	οι, ου
η =	ᾳ	η	οι, ῳ
ου =	ω	ου	ου
οι =	ῳ	οι	οι

Westcott and Hort's NT Textual Groupings:

Neutral	Alexandrian	Western	Syrian
B ℵ	A C L[e]	D L[vt] G[p]	(E F G H)[e] (HL)[a p]

a = Acts
e = Gospels
p = Paul
vt = Old Testament

FUTURE TENSE

STRUCTURES OF THE REGULAR λύω-TYPE FUTURES:

Act.: A "σ" occurs post-stem in the present active: λύ σ ω

Mid.: A "σ" occurs post-stem in the present middle: λύ σ ο μαι

Pass.: A "θη" occurs post-stem of the future middle: λύ θή σ ο μαι

Future-Perfect Passive:

    Reduplication precedes the future middle: λε λύ σ ο μαι

TRANSLATIONAL OPTIONS OF THE FUTURE INDICATIVE INTO ENGLISH:

Active: λύσεται

  he will loose

  he shall loose (emphatic)

  he will continue to loose

  (i.e., he will be loosing)

Passive: λυθήσεται

  he will be loosed

Middle: λύσεται

  he will loose himself

  he shall loose himself (emphatic)

  he will continue to loose himself

  (i.e., he will be loosing himself)

Future-Perfect Passive: λελύσεται

  he will have been loosed

USES OF THE FUTURE TENSE

1. *Punctiliar Future:* The action is conceived to be an *event* yet to happen:

   τοτέ φανήσεται τὸ σημεῖον (Matt. 24:30)

2. *Linear Future:* The action will continue throughout a future time:

   ὁ ἐναρξάμενος ἐν ὑμῖν ἔργον ἀγαθὸν ἐπιτελέσει ἄχρι ἡμέρας Χριστοῦ Ἰησοῦ (Phil. 1:6)

3. *Aphoristic Future:* The wisdom of proverbs is often future-oriented:

   ὃ γὰρ ἐὰν σπείρῃ ἄνθρωπος, τοῦτο καὶ **θερίσει** (Gal. 6:7)

   ἡ ἀλήθεια **ἐλευθερόσει** ὑμᾶς (John 8:32)

4. *Volitional Future:* The will of someone is expressed as intention or command. This use, very frequent in LXX, occurs in the NT mostly in quotations from OT.

   προσεύξομαι τῷ πνεύματι (1 Cor. 14:15); Οὐκ **ἐπιθυμήσεις** (Rom. 7:7)

5. *Periphrastic Future Construction:*

   (1) The future tense of εἰμί + a present participle:

   καὶ **ἔσεσθε μισούμενοι** ὑπὸ πάντων (Luke 21:17)

   (2) The use of some form of μέλλω + an infinitive:

   σημαίνων ποίῳ θανάτῳ **ἤμελλεν ἀποθνῄσκειν** (John 12:33)

32

Paradigms of the Future Tense

	Active	Middle	Passive	Future-Perfect Passive
I	λύ σ ω	λύ σ ο μαι	λυ θή σ ο μαι	λε λύ σ ο μαι
N	λύ σ εις	λύ σ η	λυ θή σ η	λε λύ σ η
D	λύ σ ει	λύ σ ε ται	λυ θή σ ε ται	λε λύ σ ε ται
I	λύ σ ο μεν	λυ σ ό μεθα	λυ θη σ ό μεθα	λε λυ σ ό μεθα
C	λύ σ ε τε	λύ σ ε σθε	λυ θή σ ε σθε	λε λύ σ ε σθε
A	λύ σ ουσι	λύ σ ο νται	λυ θή σ ο νται	λε λύ σ ο νται
T				
I	I shall loose	I shall loose myself	I shall be loosed	I shall have been loosed
V				
O	λύ σ οι μι	λύ σ οι μην	λυ θη σ οί μην	λε λυ σ οί μην
P	λύ σ οι ς	λύ σ οι ο	λυ θή σ οι ο	λε λύ σ οι ο
T	λύ σ οι	λύ σ οι το	λυ θή σ οι το	λε λύ σ οι το
A	λύ σ οι μεν	λυ σ οί μεθα	λυ θη σ οί μεθα	λε λυ σ οί μεθα
T	λύ σ οι τε	λύ σ οι σθε	λυ θή σ οι σθε	λε λύ σ οι σθε
I	λύ σ οι εν	λύ σ οι ντο	λυ θή σ οι ντο	λε λύ σ οι ντο
V				
E	I would loose (in indirect discourse)	I would loose myself (in indirect discourse)	I would be loosed (in indirect discourse)	I would have been loosed (in indirect discourse)

More Paradigms of the Future Tense

	Active	Middle	Passive	Future-Perfect Passive
INFINITIVE:	λύ σ ειν	λύ σ ε σθαι	λυ θή σ ε σθαι	λε λύ σ ε σθαι
PARTICIPLE:				
nom. m.s.	λύ σ ων	λυ σ ό μενος	λυ θη σ ό μενος	λε λυ σ ό μενος
nom. f.s.	λύ σ ουσα	λυ σ ο μένη	λυ θη σ ο μένη	λε λυ σ ο μένη
nom. n.s.	λῦ σ ον	λυ σ ό μενον	λυ θη σ ό μενον	λε λυ σ ό μενον

Note: The endings of all the future participles in all cases both singular and plural are exactly like those of the present participles.

Liquid-Nasal Future Tense

Structure: like regular futures except for the following:

1. omission of "σ" in the active and middle voices and "θ" in passive
2. lengthening of the variable vowels "o" to "ου" (act. & mid.)
   "ε" to "ει" (act. & mid.)
3. use of circumflex with any use of ῶ, ῇ, εῖ, or οῦ after the stem
   (exception: μενούμεθα—1p fut. mid. μένω)

Paradigms:

Active		Middle		Passive	
μενῶ	μενοῦμεν	μενοῦμαι	μενούμεθα	μενήσομαι	μενησόμεθα
μενεῖς	μενεῖτε	μενῇ	μενεῖσθε	μενήσῃ	μενήσεσθε
μενεῖ	μενοῦσι	μενεῖται	μενοῦνται	μενήσεται	μενήσονται

PERFECT TENSE

STRUCTURE OF THE PERFECT INDICATIVE:

First Perfect:

Act.: reduplication + pres. stem + κα (3s = κε) + prim. act. ends.: λέ λυ κα
-, ς, -[ε], μεν, τε, σι or ν

Mid./ reduplication + pres. stem + primary endings: **λέ λυ μαι**
Pass. μαι, σαι, ται, μεθα, σθε, νται

Second Perfect:

Act.: reduplication + pf. stem + α (3s = ε) + primary endings: πέ πονθ α (from πάσχω)

(The second perfect occurs only in the active voice:)

TRANSLATIONAL OPTIONS FOR THE PERFECT INDICATIVE:

This is the tense denoting completed action with a result existing through present time.

λέλυκε —he has loosed

λέλυται —he has loosed himself
or
—he has been loosed

πέπονθε —he has suffered; or he suffers (intensive)

USES OF THE PERFECT TENSE:

1. *Pure Perfect:* Completed action with lasting effects is emphasized:

πεπληρόκατε τὴν Ἰερουσαλὴμ τῆς διδαχῆς ὑμῶν (Acts 5:28)

2. *Intensive Perfect:* This is the strongest way of saying something *is*. This use recognizes the existing-result character of the perfect. It normally, then, is translated into English by the *present* tense.

ἡμεῖς πεπιστεύκαμεν καὶ ἐγνώκαμεν ὅτι σὺ εἶ ὁ ἅγιος τοῦ θεοῦ (John 6:69)

3. *Periphrastic Perfect Construction:* Present of εἰμί + perfect participle

πεπεισμένος γάρ ἐστιν Ἰωάννην προφήτην εἶναι (Luke 20:6)

This construction (pres. εἰμί + pf. ptc.) also holds when εἰμί is in the subjunctive mood.

οὐδεὶς δύναται ἐλθεῖν πρός με ἐὰν μὴ ᾖ δεδομένον αὐτῷ ἐκ τοῦ πατρός (John 6:65)

4. *Periphrastic Future-Perfect Construction:* Future of εἰμί + perfect participle

"The simple Future Perfect [active] does not occur in the NT" (Burton, *NTMT*, p. 45).

ὅσα ἐὰν λύσητε ἐπὶ τῆς γῆς ἔσται λελυμένα ἐν οὐρανῷ (Matt. 18:18)

36

Paradigms of the Regular (or First) Perfect Active

Indicative	Subjunctive	Optative	
λέ λυ κα	λε λύ κ ω	λε λύ κ οι μι	*Infinitive:*
λέ λυ κας	λε λύ κ ῃς	λε λύ κ οι ς	λε λυ κ έ ναι
λέ λυ κε	λε λύ κ ῃ	λε λύ κ οι	to have loosed
λε λύ κα μεν	λε λύ κ ω μεν	λε λύ κ οι μεν	
λε λύ κα τε	λε λύ κ η τε	λε λύ κ οι τε	*Participle:*
λε λύ {κα σι / κα ν}	λε λύ κ ω σι	λε λύ κ οι εν	λε λυ κ ώς nom. s.m.
			λε λυ κ υῖα nom. s.f.
			λε λυ κ ός nom. s.n.
			having loosed

I have loosed	I should (may, might) have loosed	I would have loosed (used in indirect statements); no ex. of pf. opt. [reg. or periph.] in NT

The Regular (or First) Perfect Middle or Passive

Indicative	Subjunctive	Optative
λέ λυ μαι	λε λυ μένος	λε λυ μένος
λέ λυ σαι	+ pres. subjn.	+ pres. opt. of εἰμί
λέ λυ ται	of εἰμί (= ὦ,	(= εἴην, εἴης,
λε λύ μεθα	ῇς, ῇ, ὦμεν,	εἴη, εἴημεν, εἴητε,
λέ λυ σθε	ἦτε, ὦσι)	εἴησαν)
λέ λυ νται		

I have loosed myself; I have been loosed	I should (or might) have been loosed [or] May I be loosed	I would have been loosed [or] Would that I be loosed

The Second (κ-less) Perfect of the Active Verb (πείθω)

Indicative	Subjunctive	Optative	Participle	
πέ ποιθ α	πε ποίθ ω	πε ποίθ οι μι	πε ποιθ ώς	nom. s.m.
πέ ποιθ ας	πε ποίθ ῃς	πε ποίθ οι ς	πε ποιθ υῖα	nom. s.f.
πέ ποιθ ε	πε ποίθ ῃ	πε ποίθ οι	πε ποιθ ός	nom. s.n.
πε ποίθ α μεν	πε ποίθ ω μεν	πε ποίθ οι μεν	having trusted in . . .	
πε ποίθ α τε	πε ποίθ η τε	πε ποίθ οι τε		
πε ποίθ α σι	πε ποίθ ω σι	πε ποίθ οι εν		
I have trusted in . . .	I should have trusted in . . .	I would have trusted in . . .		

Rules for Reduplication:

χ reduplicates as	κεχ
φ "	πεφ
θ "	τεθ
σ "	εσ [exc.=σέσωκα]
ζ "	εξ < σῴζω
ξ "	εξ

Contractions: verb stems ending in a mute:

at soft palate (velar)	κ, γ, χ	+ σ	=	ξ
at teeth (dental)	τ, δ, θ, ζ	+ σ	=	σ
at lips (labial)	π, β, φ	+ σ	=	ψ
	κ, γ, χ	+ θ	=	χθ
	τ, δ, θ, ζ	+ θ	=	σθ
	π, ν, γ	+ θ	=	φθ

PLUPERFECT TENSE

STRUCTURE OF THE PLUPERFECT INDICATIVE:

Act.: augment + reduplication + pres. stem + κει + sec. act. ends. = ἐ λε λύ κει ν

Mid./
Pass.: { augment + reduplication + pres. stem + sec. mid. ends. = ἐ λε λύ μην

Second Pluperfect: In analogy to the second perfect, certain irregular verbs like οἶδα [second pf.], ᾔδειν [second plupf.] omit or compress the augment and reduplication, having a pf. stem (instead of pres.) and omit the κ before the secondary endings.

Pluperfects occur only in the indicative mood.

TRANSLATIONAL OPTIONS AND COMPLETE PARADIGMS OF THE PLUPERFECT:

Active		Middle/Passive	
ἐ λε λύ κει ν		ἐ λε λύ μην	
ἐ λέ λύ κει ς		ἐ λέ λυ σο	
ἐ λε λύ κει	he had loosed	ἐ λέ λυ το	he had loosed himself
ἐ λε λύ κει μεν		ἐ λε λύ μεθα	[or] he had been loosed
ἐ λε λύ κει τε		ἐ λέ λυ σθε	
ἐ λε λύ κει σαν		ἐ λέ λυ ντο	

USES OF THE PLUPERFECT TENSE:

The pluperfect is the *perfect indicative of past time*; therefore, the uses of this tense are comparable to those of the perfect tense.

1. *Pure Pluperfect:* The basic pluperfect expresses completed action with a resultant state as occurring in past time:

Μαρίᾳ τῇ Μαγδαληνῇ, παρ' ἧς ἐκβεβλήκει ἑπτὰ δαιμόνια (Mark 16:9)

2. *Intensive Pluperfect:* As does the perfect, this use emphasizes a completion whose continued state still stands, making a translation into English in the *present* tense appropriate. (It suits well verbs of seeing, knowing, understanding, and believing.)

παρέθεντο αὐτοὺς τῷ κυρίῳ εἰς ὃν πεπιστεύκεισαν (Acts 14:23)

3. *Periphrastic Pluperfect Construction:* imperfect of εἰμί + perfect participle

The pluperfect meaning (pure or intensive) is achieved without the use of the pluperfect tense:

καὶ γυναῖκές τινες αἳ ἦσαν τεθεραπευμέναι (Luke 8:2)

MOOD

Mood signifies (by its conjugational forms) the *manner* by which predication is made.

1. *Definite predication* = Indicative mood; used in any tense.

ἔρχονται πρὸς τὸν Ἰησοῦν (Mark 5:15); οὐ γὰρ ἔστιν ἐξουσία . . . (Rom. 13:1)

2. *Indefinite predication* is uncertain and contingent:

(1) Subjunctive mood: used only in the present, aorist, and perfect tenses:

ἐὰν ὑμεῖς **μείνητε** ἐν τῷ λόγῳ τῷ ἐμῷ . . . (John 8:31)

(2) Optative mood: 1—is found infrequently in the NT to show even more remote indefiniteness than the subjunctive:

2—is used in the present, future, aorist, perfect, and future-perfect tenses:

γένοιτό μοι κατὰ τὸ ῥῆμά σου (Luke 1:38)

3. *Volitional predication* = Optative mood occasionally (as in the example just given);
Imperative mood: used only in the imperative present and aorist tenses:

χαίρετε ἐν κυρίῳ (Phil. 3:1); μηκέτι **ἁμάρτανε** (John 5:14)

While the next two categories of verb analysis are not properly "moods" according to the grammarians, they exist as forms of predication not altogether different from a mood. When parsing, one recognizes them as if they were moods (by saying Infinitive or Participle instead of Indicative, Subjunctive, Optative, or Imperative).

4. *Unlimited predication* = Infinitive ['not finite] "mood"; used in the present, future, aorist, perfect, and future-perfect tenses:

ἰδοὺ ἐξῆλθεν ὁ σπείρων τοῦ **σπείρειν** (Matt. 13:3)

5. *Associated predication* = Participle; used in every tense but the imperfect and the pluperfect, and having declensional endings like a noun or adjective:

περὶ τοῦ υἱοῦ αὐτοῦ τοῦ **γενομένου** ἐκ σπέρματος Δαυίδ (Rom. 1:3)

Because of the versatility of the participle the verbal idea may be expressed not as action but substantivally as *one* who acts or is acted upon:

πᾶς ὁ **θεωρῶν** τὸν υἱὸν καὶ **πιστεύων** εἰς αὐτὸν ἔχῃ ζωὴν αἰώνιον (John 6:40)

Ἤκουσεν δὲ Ἡρῴδης . . . τὰ **γινόμενα** πάντα (Luke 9:7)

42

THE FUNCTIONS OF MOOD

THE INDICATIVE MOOD:

Basic Idea: sure, real, definite predication: certainty of assertion

1. *Statement:*

   Οὐ θέλομεν δὲ ὑμᾶς ἀγνοεῖν (1 Thess. 4:13)

2. *Interrogation:*

   κύριε, ποῦ ὑπάγεις; (John 13:36)

3. *Imperative:*

   The future tense, second person, can provide a command (e.g., the Decalog in the LXX).

   οὐκ ἐκπειράσεις κύριον τὸν θεόν σου (Matt. 4:7)

4. *Assumptive assertion:* (Reality is assumed for the sake of argument.) In first and second class conditions (either protasis or apodosis) the indicative mood operates with "real" assumptions, but the contingency of the conditional structure predominates in translation:

   εἰ {ἐγνώκατέ [p66, א] με, καὶ τὸν πατέρα μου ἄν {γνώσεσθε [p66, א, D]
   {ἐγνώκειτε [A, B]   {ᾔδειτε [B] (John 14:7)

Basic Principle of Parsing: Only the Indicative has augments.

THE SUBJUNCTIVE MOOD:

Basic Idea: contingency, uncertain fulfillment

1. *Subjunctive with* ἵνα *and* ὅπως *clauses:*

The subjunctive occurs characteristically with these two conjunctions. (However, ἵνα occurs with the indicative about two dozen times in NT.)

(1) *Purpose:*

Ἐκζητήσατε τὸ καλὸν καὶ μὴ τὸ πονηρόν, ὅπως **ζήσητε** (Amos 5:14, LXX)

Ἐβάστασαν πάλιν λίθους οἱ Ἰουδαῖοι ἵνα **λιθάσωσιν** αὐτόν (John 10:31)

Negative Purpose: ἵνα μή + subjunctive = "lest"

γρηγορεῖτε καὶ προσεύχεσθε, ἵνα μὴ **ἔλθητε** εἰς πειρασμόν (Mark 14:38)

(2) *Result:*

τίς ἥμαρτεν . . . ἵνα τυφλὸς **γεννηθῇ**; (John 9:2)

(3) *Indirect Command:*

Διαμαρτύρομαι . . . ἵνα ταῦτα **φυλάξῃς** (1 Tim. 5:21)

Indirect Command (Negative) = Prohibition: ἵνα + neg. pron. + subjn. + neg.

παρήγγειλεν αὐτοῖς ἵνα μηδὲν **αἴρωσιν** . . . μὴ ἄρτον (Mark 6:8)

(4) *Wish:*

πληρώσατέ μου τὴν χαρὰν ἵνα τὸ αὐτὸ **φρονῆτε** (Phil. 2:2)

SUBJUNCTIVE MOOD (CONT.)

2. *Subjunctive with Protases of Class Three Conditions (ἐὰν and ἐὰν μή):*

κἀγὼ ἐὰν **ὑψωθῶ** ἐκ τῆς γῆς, πάντας ἑλκύσω πρὸς ἐμαυτόν (John 12:32)

3. *Subjunctive with Indefinite Relative Clauses with ἄν or ἐάν:*

ὅ τι ἄν **λέγῃ** ὑμῖν ποιήσατε (John 2:5)
ὅσα ἄν **αἰτήσῃ** τὸν θεὸν δώσει σοι ὁ θεός (John 11:22)
εἰς ἣν δ᾽ ἄν πόλιν ἢ κώμην **εἰσέλθητε**, . . . (Matt. 10:11)
ὅπου ἐὰν **κηρυχθῇ** τὸ εὐαγγέλιον . . . ὃ ἐποίησεν αὕτη λαληθήσεται (Mark 14:9)

4. *Subjunctive with Temporal Clauses with ἄν:*

ὅταν [ὅτε + ἄν] **ἔλθῃ** ἐκεῖνος, ἀναγγελεῖ ἡμῖν ἅπαντα (John 4:25)
ἕως ἄν **ἴδωσιν** τὸν υἱὸν τοῦ ἀνθρώπου (Matt. 16:28)
τὰ δὲ λοιπὰ ὡς ἄν **ἔλθω** διατάξομαι (1 Cor. 11:34)
μὴ ἰδεῖν θάνατον πρὶν [ἢ] ἄν **ἴδῃ** τὸν χριστόν (Luke 2:26)

5. *Hortatory Subjunctive: First Person Plural Exhortations:* "Let us . . ."

Μηκέτι οὖν ἀλλήλους **κρίνωμεν** (Rom. 14:13)
Σπουδάσωμεν οὖν εἰσελθεῖν εἰς ἐκείνην τὴν κατάπαυσιν (Heb. 4:11)

6. *Subjunctive with Second and Third Person Prohibitions of the Aorist Tense:*

This use of the subjunctive forbids in advance the contemplated action: "Do not begin to . . ."

μὴ **σκληρύνητε** τὰς καρδίας ὑμῶν (Heb. 3:8)
μὴ τίς με **δόξῃ** ἄφρονα εἶναι· (2 Cor. 11:16)
καὶ μὴ **ὑπερίδῃς** τὴν μητέρα σου (Tobit 4:3)

7. *Subjunctive with Emphatic Denials of Futurity* (οὐ μή always used):

οὐ μή with the aorist subjunctive occurs in 86% of NT uses, and οὐ μή with the future indicative for the rest; Job 23:11 LXX has οὐ μή ἐκκλίνω (a futuristic present) ἀπὸ ἐνταλμάτων αὐτοῦ.

The aorist subjunctive and future indicative are used interchangeably:

ὁ ἐρχόμενος πρὸς ἐμὲ οὐ μὴ **πεινάσῃ**,
καὶ ὁ πιστεύων εἰς ἐμὲ οὐ μὴ **διψήσει** πώποτε (John 6:35)

8. *Subjunctive with Deliberations:*

The subjunctive is ideal for consideration of a future course of action and the decisions those actions will involve. (The future indicative also can be used for contemplation of the future, but with more certainty—Rom. 8:31, 33.)

Νῦν ἡ ψυχή μου τετάρακται, καὶ τί **εἴπω**; (John 12:27)
Τί οὖν; **ἁμαρτήσομεν**, ὅτι οὐκ ἐσμὲν ὑπὸ νόμον ἀλλὰ ὑπὸ χάριν; (Rom. 6:15)

THE OPTATIVE MOOD:

Basic idea: contingent possibility weaker than the subjunctive; there are only about 68 optatives used in the NT.

1. *Volition:* (expression of a wish) About 38 optative volitions occur in NT.

μὴ γένοιτο (Rom. 6:2 and in 14 other instances)
"May it not be so!"   "By no means!"   "Let it never happen!"

χάρις ὑμῖν καὶ εἰρήνη πληθυνθείη (1 Peter 1:2)

2. *Imprecation:* (a negative volition tantamount to a curse)

μηκέτι εἰς τὸν αἰῶνα ἐκ σοῦ μηδεὶς καρπὸν φάγοι (Mark 11:14)
τὸ ἀργύριόν σου σὺν σοὶ εἴη [pres. opt. act. 3s εἰμί] εἰς ἀπώλειαν (Acts. 8:20)

3. *Protasis of a Class Four Condition:* ("should" or "would")

ἀλλ᾽ εἰ καὶ πάσχοιτε διὰ δικαιοσύνην, μακάριοι (1 Peter 3:14)

4. *Potentiality:* ("could" or "would")

This potential use as a weakened subjunctive will sometimes be expressed instead by the subjunctive or even the future indicative.

πῶς γὰρ ἂν δυναίμην ἐὰν μή τις ὁδηγήσει με; (Acts 8:31)
εἴ πως δύναιντο καταντήσαντες εἰς Φοίνικα (Acts 27:12)

5. *Deliberation:* ("might," "would," "could")

τινες ἔλεγον· τί ἂν θέλοι ὁ σπερμολόγος οὗτος λέγειν; (Acts 17:18)

THE IMPERATIVE MOOD:

Basic idea: The first person expresses volition toward the second person, and sometimes [in Greek, but not in English] toward the third person.

1. *Command:* σεαυτὸν ἁγνὸν **τήρει** (1 Tim. 5:22)

2. *Prohibition:* (μή + imperative [usually present tense])

   εἴ τις οὐ θέλει ἐργάζεσθαι μηδὲ **ἐσθιέτω** (2 Thess. 3:10)

3. *Request:* **ποίησόν** με ὡς ἕνα τῶν μισθίων σου (Luke 15:19)

4. *Permission:* εἰ δὲ ὁ ἄπιστος χωρίζεται, **χωριζέσθω** (1 Cor. 7:15)

5. *Admonition:* (warning) **βλέπετε** τοὺς κακοὺς ἐργάτας (Phil. 3:2)

6. *Exhortation:* (encouragement) **δίδοτε**, καὶ δοθήσεται ὑμῖν (Luke 6:38)

7. *Confrontation:* **δεῖξόν** μοι τὴν πίστιν σου χωρὶς τῶν ἔργων (James 2:18)

Translational Options for Third-Person Imperatives:

ἀσθενεῖ τις . . . **προσκαλεσάσθω** τοὺς πρεσβυτέρους . . . καὶ **προσευξάσθωσαν** (James 5:14: "have him call," "he should call," "he must call," "let him call" . . . "have them pray")

48

IMPERATIVE MOOD (CONT.)

POSSIBLE ALTERNATIVES TO THE IMPERATIVE MOOD

1. *Uses of the Future Indicative as a Command:*

   κύριον τὸν θεόν σου **προσκυνήσεις** (Luke 4:8)

2. *Use of μή and 2nd or 3rd Person Aorist Subjunctive as a Prohibition:*

   μή τις οὖν αὐτὸν **ἐξουθενήσῃ** (1 Cor. 16:11)

3. *Use of a Volitional Optative, Especially of an Imprecation:*

   μηκέτι εἰς τὸν αἰῶνα ἐκ σοῦ μηδεὶς καρπὸν **φάγοι** (Mark 11:14)

4. *Use of the Infinitive as a Command:*

   Δούλους ἰδίοις δεσπόταις **ὑποτάσσεσθαι** ἐν πᾶσιν (Titus 2:9)

5. *Use of the Participle as an Exhortation:*

   τῇ ἐλπίδι **χαίροντες** [See context.] (Rom. 12:12)

Catchy Imperatives Parsed and Correlated

λῦσον: 1Aor/Act 2s (or Fut/Ptc/Act Nom s n);   λύου: Prs/Mid 2s;   λιποῦ 2 Aor/Mid 2s

λῦσαι: 1Aor/Mid 2s (or 1 Aor/Inf/Act);   λάλει: Prs/Act 2s from λαλέω

λύθητι: 1Aor/Pas 2s;   λίπηθι: 2 Aor/Pas 2s;   πλάνα Prs/Act 2s from πλανάω

λυθήτω: 1 Aor/Pas 3s;   λιπήτω 2 Aor/Pas 3s;   πλανῶ Prs/Mid 2s from πλανάω

PROHIBITIONS

There are two perspectives utilized in prohibitions with an initial μή:

1. *Cease from an action in progress:* μή + present imperative:
   "Do not continue . . . Stop . . . Cease . . . Quit . . . "

μὴ φοβοῦ, μόνον πίστευσον, καὶ σωθήσεται (Luke 8:50)
Μὴ δοκεῖτε ὅτι ἐγὼ κατηγορήσω ὑμῶν πρὸς τὸν πατέρα (John 5:45)

2. *Do not begin an anticipated action:* μή + aorist subjunctive

   "Do not begin to . . . Do not start to . . . "

Μὴ νομίσητε ὅτι ἦλθον καταλῦσαι τὸν νόμον (Matt. 5:17)
Μὴ οὖν φοβηθῆτε αὐτούς (Matt. 10:26)

Note on other prohibitions: If the μή comes *after* the imperative, the fine distinctions above do not apply. In such a case the μή makes negative what follows it, rather than keying directly on the verb.

ἐργάζεσθε μὴ τὴν βρῶσιν τὴν ἀπολλυμένην ἀλλὰ . . . (John 6:27)

The translation of such a construction is necessarily more ambiguous: "Work not for . . . " or "Do not labor for. . . ." If μή *precedes* a verb other than the present imperative or the aorist subjunctive the ambiguity follows: μὴ ὀμόσαι (Matt. 5:34) "Do not take an oath."

THE INFINITIVE

Not properly a mood, the infinitive nevertheless has voice and tense and is parsed as a mood. It functions to express action without the limitations of personal endings. About one in 60 words in NT is an infinitive.

USES OF THE INFINITIVE:

1. *Substantival:*

(1) *Subject of a finite verb:* ἀπόκειται τοῖς ἀνθρώποις ἅπαξ **ἀποθανεῖν** (Heb. 9:27)

(2) *Object of a finite verb:* μή τις ἤνεγκεν αὐτῷ **φαγεῖν**; (John 4:33)

(3) *Predicate complement:* Σίμων, ἔχω σοί τι **εἰπεῖν** (Luke 7:40)

(4) *Object of a preposition:* λέγω ὑμῖν πρὸ τοῦ **γενέσθαι** (John 13:19)

(5) *Appositive:* Τοῦτο γάρ ἐστιν θέλημα τοῦ θεοῦ, ὁ ἁγιασμὸς ὑμῶν, **ἀπέχεσθαι** ὑμᾶς ἀπὸ τῆς πορνείας (1 Thess. 4:3)

(6) *Salutation* = formal greetings = English: "Greetings," "Good Day!"

Ἰάκωβος . . . δώδεκα φυλαῖς ταῖς ἐν τῇ διασπορᾷ **χαίρειν** (James 1:1)

2. *Adverbial:*

(1) *Purpose:* ἵνα ἀποστέλλῃ αὐτοὺς **κηρύσσειν** (Mark 3:14)

(2) *Result:* ἔδωκεν αὐτοῖς ἐξουσίαν πνευμάτων ἀκαθάρτων ὥστε **ἐκβάλλειν** αὐτὰ (Matt. 10:1) θεὸς γάρ ἐστιν ὁ ἐνεργῶν ἐν ὑμῖν καὶ τὸ **θέλειν** καὶ τὸ **ἐνεργεῖν** ὑμὲρ τῆς εὐδοκίας (Phil. 2:13)

(3) *Adjectival Complement:* οὐκέτι εἰμὶ ἄξιος **κληθῆναι** υἱός σου (Luke 15:19)

3. *Verbal Complement:* Certain verbs need an infinitive to complete them:

μέλλω, δύναμαι, ὀφείλω, δεῖ, θέλω, ζητέω, ἔξεστιν, ἄρχω, πρέπω.

πῶς δύνασθε ἀγαθὰ **λαλεῖν**; (Matt. 12:34)

4. *Finite Verb:* When so used, as in *indirect discourse,* the person and number can be supplied from the context.

ὁ ἀποκτείνας ὑμᾶς δόξῃ λατρείαν **προσφέρειν** τῷ θεῷ (John 16:2) οὐκ ἔσχηκα ἄνεσιν τῷ πνεύματί μου τῷ μὴ **εὑρεῖν** με Τίτον (2 Cor. 2:13)

5. *Imperative:* **κλαίειν** μετὰ κλαιόντων (Rom. 12:15) [rare in NT]

6. *Adjectival:* καθὼς ἔθος ἐστὶν τοῖς Ἰουδαίοις **ἐνταφιάζειν** (John 19:40)

(This infinitive modifies ἔθος.) [rare in NT]

7. *Infinitive Absolute:* καὶ ὡς ἔπος **εἰπεῖν** (Heb. 7:9) [rare in NT]

52

SPECIAL CONSTRUCTION OF THE INFINITIVE AND A REFERENTIAL ACCUSATIVE:

Frequently in good Greek the infinitive is accompanied by an *accusative of general reference*. Such referenced accusatives function as subjects of infinitival action. Subjects of infinitives occur only in the accusative case.

ὥστε **δουλεύειν ἡμᾶς** ἐν καινότητι πνεύματος (Rom. 7:6) [use: result clause]

Τοῖς δὲ γεγαμηκόσιν παραγγέλλω . . . **γυναῖκα** ἀπὸ ἀνδρὸς μὴ **χωρισθῆναι** (1 Cor. 7:10) [use: imperative]

καὶ ἐν τῷ **σπείρειν αὐτὸν** . . . (Luke 8:5) [use: temporal clause]

ἐκεῖνον δεῖ **αὐξάνειν, ἐμὲ** δὲ **ἐλαττοῦσθαι** (John 3:30) [use: verbal complements]

ὁ οὖν ὄχλος ὁ ἑστὼς καὶ ἀκούσας ἔλεγεν **βροντὴν γεγονέναι** (John 12:29) [use: finite verb in an indirect statement]

Caution: Not every accusative noun with an infinitive is an accusative of general reference. The use may be that of the direct object of the verbal idea in the infinitive as in (John 6:21): ἤθελον οὖν λαβεῖν αὐτὸν . . . or (Matt. 23:23): ταῦτα [δὲ] ἔδει ποιῆσαι. . . .

The accusative of general reference, the direct object accusative and the accusative of double direct object can all accompany the same infinitive:

διαπονούμενοι διὰ τὸ διδάσκειν {αὐτοὺς τὸν {λαὸν . . . τὴν {ἀνάστασιν (Acts 4:2)

Gen.Ref. D.O. D.D.O.

INFINITIVAL FORMS:

Infinitives are easy to recognize structurally because, taking the form appropriate to their tense and voice, they all have one of the following endings:

-ειν, -αι, -ναι, -σθαι

except for contract verbs that have:

ᾶν, εῖν, οῦν in the present

Active Voice:

Present	Future	1 Aorist	2 Aorist	Perfect
λύ ειν	λύσ ειν	λῦσ αι	λιπ εῖν	λελυκέ ναι

Middle Voice:

Present	Future	1 Aorist	2 Aorist	Perfect
λύε σθαι	λύσε σθαι	λύσα σθαι	λιπέ σθαι	λελύ σθαι

Passive Voice:

Future	Future Perfect	1 Aorist	2 Aorist
λυθήσε σθαι	λελύσε σθαι	λυθῆ ναι	λιπῆ ναι

There are no augments because only the indicative has an augment.

THE PARTICIPLE

The Greek participle is the most versatile of the Greek verb forms and one of the distinctives of the language. As a verb, it has voice and tense. It occurs in all voices and all tenses except the imperfect and pluperfect. In place of personal endings the participle has declensional inflections that give it gender, number, and one of the inflectional cases common to a noun or adjective. The participle readily serves in these various ways: as a substantive, adverb, adjective, finite verb, or imperative. A participle of a transitive verb can take a direct object just as can the infinitive. On average every twenty-first word in the NT is a participle.

THE FUNCTIONS OF THE PARTICIPLE

SUBSTANTIVAL PARTICIPLES:

(1) *Subject:* ὁ τὸν λόγον μου **ἀκούων** καὶ **πιστεύων** τῷ πέμψαντί με ἔχει ζωὴν αἰώνιον (John 5:24)

(2) *Predicate Nominative:* τὸ πνεῦμά ἐστιν τὸ **ζῳοποιοῦν** (John 6:63)

(3) *Direct Object:* τὸν **ἐρχόμενον** πρός ἐμὲ οὐ μὴ ἐκβάλω ἔξω (John 6:37)

(4) *Objective Complement.* This use indicates the *action itself*, especially after verbs of perception. (Do not confuse this use, complementing the *object* of the finite verb, with that use complementing the verb—i.e., Verbal Complement.)

Ἰησοῦς οὖν ὡς εἶδεν αὐτὴν **κλαίουσαν** (John 11:33)

(5) *Indirect Object:*

τῷ δὲ **ἐργαζομένῳ** ὁ μισθὸς οὐ λογίζεται κατὰ χάριν (Rom. 4:4)

(6) *Object of a Preposition:*

διὰ τοῦ **ἐνοικοῦντος** αὐτοῦ πνεύματος ἐν ὑμῖν (Rom. 8:11)

(7) *Appositive:* κύριος ὁ θεός, ὁ ὢν . . . καὶ ὁ **ἐρχόμενος** (Rev. 1:8)

ADVERBIAL PARTICIPLES:

The adverbial participle modifies the main verb of the sentence in a manner that can be deduced from the context. *Proper supporting terms, therefore, can be supplied in an English translation in order to indicate such an adverbial relationship.*

(1) *Purpose:* ("for," "for the purpose of," "in order that/to," "to")

γυναῖκες . . . ἠκολούθησαν τῷ Ἰησοῦ . . . **διακονοῦσαι** αὐτῷ (Matt. 27:55)

(2) *Result:* ("so as to," "with the effect of," "resulting in . . .")

καὶ αὐτὸς ἐδίδασκεν ἐν ταῖς συναγωγαῖς αὐτῶν, **δοξαζόμενος** ὑπὸ πάντων (Luke 4:15)

(3) *Time:* ("when," "while," "after," "as")

Ἀπολυθέντες δὲ ἦλθον πρὸς τοὺς ἰδίους (Acts 4:23)

(4) *Cause:* ("because," "since")

ἐχάρησαν οὖν οἱ μαθηταὶ **ἰδόντες** τὸν κύριον (John 20:20)

(5) *Condition:* ("if")

Ταῦτα ὑποτιθέμενος τοῖς ἀδελφοῖς καλὸς ἔσῃ διάκονος Χριστοῦ Ἰησοῦ (1 Tim. 4:6) ἐλπὶς δὲ βλεπομένη οὐκ ἔστιν ἐλπίς (Rom. 8:24)

(6) *Concession:* ("though," "although")

δι᾽ ὅλης νυκτὸς κοπιάσαντες οὐδὲν ἐλάβομεν (Luke 5:5)

(7) *Means:* ("by," "by means of")

μᾶλλον δὲ προσετίθεντο πιστεύοντες τῷ κυρίῳ (Acts 5:14)

(8) *Manner:* ("in" "in a manner of _____," "_____ly")

καὶ ἕτερα πολλὰ βλασφημοῦντες ἔλεγον εἰς αὐτόν (Luke 22:65)

Note: Some grammarians prefer to combine means and manner as a composite category. Likewise this use is somewhat ambiguous with the *Unrestricted* category that follows, because "manner" is practically synonymous with the pure adverbial idea.

(9) *Unrestricted:* (uses no adverbial auxiliaries)

The adverbial use of the participial clause converts into good English satisfactorily without any of the supplementary words common to uses 1–8. This *adverbially unrestricted use of the participle* is not far from the VERBAL use: Coordinate with a Finite Verb.

κατὰ πίστιν ἀπέθανον οὗτοι πάντες, μὴ λαβόντες τὰς ἐπαγγελίας ἀλλὰ πόρρωθεν αὐτὰς ἰδόντες καὶ ἀσπασάμενοι καὶ ὁμολογήσαντες ὅτι ξένοι καὶ παρεπίδημοί εἰσιν ἐπὶ τῆς γῆς (Heb. 11:13).

Note on Genitive Absolutes:

Genitive absolutes regularly employ an *adverbial* determination of the participle in one of these nine ways just illustrated.

ADJECTIVAL PARTICIPLES:

(1) *Ascriptive Attributive:* The adjectival participle occurs anarthrously somewhere after the word it modifies, or it comes before the word it modifies, but always without an *intervening* article.

καθὼς ἀπέστειλέν με ὁ ζῶν πατήρ (John 6:57)

ὅμοιός ἐστιν ἀνθρώπῳ **οἰκοδομοῦντι** οἰκίαν (Luke 6:48)

(2) *Restrictive Attributive:* The order for emphatic distinctiveness is:

article + noun + article + participle.

Translate this construction into English by a restrictive relative clause or by an adjective.

ἐργάζεσθε μὴ τὴν βρῶσιν τὴν **ἀπολλυμένην**, ἀλλὰ τὴν βρῶσιν τὴν **μένουσαν** εἰς ζωὴν αἰώνιον (John 6:27)

(3) *Predicate Attributive:* With the verb "to be" the participle functions in the predicate as a predicate adjective.

ἄνδρες φέροντες ἐπὶ κλίνης ἄνθρωπον ὃς ἦν **παραλελυμένος** (Luke 5:18)

VERBAL PARTICIPLES:

(1) *Coordinate with a Finite Verb:* The participle is translated as a finite verb in parallel to the main verb of the sentence.

Ὁ δὲ Ἰωάννης ἀκούσας ἐν τῷ δεσμωτηρίῳ τὰ ἔργα τοῦ Χριστοῦ **πέμψας** διὰ τῶν μαθητῶν αὐτοῦ εἶπεν αὐτῷ (Matt. 11:2, 3).

(2) *Complementary with certain verbs:* The participle is necessary to complete the idea of the main verb:

1—*Complement proper:*

οὐ παυόμεθα ὑπὲρ ὑμῶν **προσευχόμενοι** (Col. 1:9)

2—*Complementary periphrastic:* The participle complements the verb *to be* in one of its tenses. Examples are found in this *Enchiridion* under the Periphrastic Present, Periphrastic Imperfect, Periphrastic Future, Periphrastic Perfect, and Periphrastic Pluperfect.

(3) *Imperatival:* The participle also has an imperatival function, not frequently used.

1—*Single imperative:*

εἰ δυνατὸν τὸ ἐξ ὑμῶν, μετὰ πάντων ἀνθρώπων **εἰρηνεύοντες** (Rom. 12:18).

2—*Coordinate imperative:* The participle is coordinate with an imperative:

πορευθέντες ἀπαγγείλατε Ἰωάννῃ ἃ ἀκούετε καὶ βλέπετε (Matt. 11:4).

SAMPLE TEXT FROM CODEX VATICANUS (FOURTH CENTURY)

Κ ΤΟΝΜΕΝΠΡΩΤΟΝΛΟΓΟΝ
ΕΠΟΙΗϹΑΜΗΝΠΕΡΙΠΑΝΤω
ωΘΕΟΦΙΛΕωΝΗΡΞΑΤΟ
ΙϹΠΟΙΕΙΝΤΕΚΑΙΔΙΔΑϹΚΙ
ΑΧΡΙΗϹΗΜΕΡΑϹΕΝΤΕΙΛΑ
ΜΕΝΟϹΤΟΙϹΑΠΟϹΤΟΛΟΙϹ
ΔΙΑΠΝΕΥΜΑΤΟϹΑΓΙΟΥΟΥϹ
ΕΞΕΛΕΞΑΤΟΑΝΕΛΗΜΦθΗ·

ΕϹΤΙ ΔΕΚΑΙΑΛΛΑΠΟΛΛΑΑΕΠΟΙ
ΗϹΕΝΟΙϹΑΤΙΝΑΕΑΝΓΡΑ
φΗΤΑΙΚΑΘΕΝΟΥΔΑΥΤο
ΟΙΜΑΙΤΟΝΚΟϹΜΟΝΧω
ΡΗϹΕΙΝΤΑΓΡΑφΟΜΕΝΑ
ΒΙΒΛΙΑ : ·,·—

Key Declensions of the Active Participle

PRESENT

	M	F	N	M	F	N
N	λύων	λύουσα	λῦον	λύοντες	λύουσαι	λύοντα
G	λύοντος	λυούσης	λύοντος	λυόντων	λυουσῶν	λυόντων
D	λύοντι	λυούσῃ	λύοντι	λύουσι	λυούσαις	λύουσι
A	*λύοντα*	λύουσαν	λῦον	λύοντας	λυούσας	*λύοντα*

FIRST AORIST

	M	F	N	M	F	N
N	λύσας	λύσασα	λῦσαν	λύσαντες	λύσασαι	λύσαντα
G	λύσαντος	λυσάσης	λύσαντος	λυσάντων	λυσασῶν	λυσάντων
D	λύσαντι	λυσάσῃ	λύσαντι	λύσασι	λυσάσαις	λύσασι
A	*λύσαντα*	λύσασαν	λῦσαν	λύσαντας	λυσάσας	*λύσαντα*

FIRST PERFECT

	M	F	N	M	F	N
N	λελυκώς	λελυκυῖα	λελυκός	λελυκότες	λελυκυῖαι	λελυκότα
G	λελυκότος	λελυκυίας	λελυκότος	λελυκότων	λελυκυιῶν	λελυκότων
D	λελυκότι	λελυκυίᾳ	λελυκότι	λελυκόσι	λελυκυίαις	λελυκόσι
A	*λελυκότα*	λελυκυῖαν	λελυκός	λελυκότας	λελυκυίας	λελυκότα

Key Declension of the Middle Participle

λυόμενος	λυομένη	λυόμενα	λυόμενοι	λυόμεναι	λυόμενα
λυομένου	λυομένης	λυομένην	λυομένων	λυομένων	λυομένων
λυομένῳ	λυομένῃ	λυομένῳ	λυομένοις	λυομέναις	λυομένοις
λυόμενον	λυομένην	λυομένην	λυομένους	λυομένας	λυόμενα

(P R E S E N T)

Key Declension of the Passive Participle

λυθείς	λυθεῖσα	λυθέν	λυθέντες	λυθεῖσαι	*λυθέντα*
λυθέντος	λυθείσης	λυθέντος	λυθέντων	λυθεισῶν	λυθέντων
λυθέντι	λυθείσῃ	λυθέντι	λυθεῖσι	λυθείσαις	λυθεῖσι
λυθέντα	λυθεῖσαν	λυθέν	λυθέντας	λυθείσας	*λυθέντα*

(A O R I S T)

Notes on Participial Forms

1. By use of the Key Declensions with the characteristic tense structures one can parse any participle.
2. The future participle is very rare in LXX and NT (Robertson, *GGNTLHR*, p. 374): Matt. 27:49.
3. Ambiguous participles on these last two pages have been specially marked by italicizing.

2
NOUNS, CASE USAGE, PRONOUNS

DECLENSIONS OF NOUNS

Key to lines: 1 = nominative; 2 = genitive; 3 = dative; 4 = accusative; 5 = vocative. Vocative forms are included only if different from the nominative. Plurals follow on line their singular form. Articles denote gender. One space is skipped before each ending to differentiate it. Certain endings are italicized to denote their distinctiveness.

SECOND DECLENSION:

1	ὁ	φίλ ος	φίλ οι	ἡ	ὁδ ός	ὁδ οί	τὸ	ἔργ ον	ἔργ α
2		φίλ ου	φίλ ων		ὁδ οῦ	ὁδ ῶν		ἔργ ου	ἔργ ων
3		φίλ ῳ	φίλ οις		ὁδ ῷ	ὁδ οῖς		ἔργ ῳ	ἔργ οις
4		φίλ ον	φίλ ους		ὁδ όν	ὁδ ούς		ἔργ ον	ἔργ α
5		φίλ ε			way			work	
		friend							

Compare variations in irregular *adjective* (masc. and neut.): διπλοῦς, ῆ, οῦν

1	διπλ οῦς	διπλ οῖ	διπλ οῦν	διπλ ᾶ
2	διπλ οῦ	διπλ ῶν	διπλ οῦ	διπλ ῶν
3	διπλ ῷ	διπλ οῖς	διπλ ῷ	διπλ οῖς
4	διπλ οῦν	διπλ οῦς	διπλ οῦν	διπλ ᾶ
	double, twofold, twice			

FIRST DECLENSION:

nom. s. in α:

1	ἡ	γλῶσσ α	γλῶσσ αι	ἡ	ἡμέρ α	ἡμέρ αι
2		γλώσσ ης	γλωσσ ῶν		ἡμέρ ας	ἡμερ ῶν
3		γλώσσ ῃ	γλώσσ αις		ἡμέρ ᾳ	ἡμέρ αις
4		γλῶσσ αν	γλῶσσ ας		ἡμέρ αν	ἡμέρ ας
		tongue, language			day	

nom. s. in ας:

				nom. s. in η			nom. s. in ης		
1	ὁ	νεανί ας	νεανί αι	ἡ	γ ῆ	——	ὁ	κριτ ής	κριτ αί
2		νεανί ου	νεανί ῶν		γ ῆς	——		κριτ οῦ	κριτ ῶν
3		νεανί ᾳ	νεανί αις		γ ῇ	——		κριτ ῇ	κριτ αῖς
4		νεανί αν	νεανί ας		γ ῆν	——		κριτ ήν	κριτ άς
5		νεανί α			earth			judge	
		young man							

THIRD DECLENSION NOUNS:

The base (or stem) is determined from the gen. sing. less the ending.

Base ending in λ or ρ:

1	ὁ	ἄνδρ ες	ἡ	χεῖρ	χεῖρ ες
1	ὁ ἀνήρ	ἄνδρ ες	ἡ χείρ		χεῖρ ες
2	ἀνδρ ός	ἄνδρ ῶν	χειρ ός		χειρ ῶν
3	ἀνδρ ί	ἄνδρ άσι	χειρ ί		χερ σί
4	ἄνδρ α	ἄνδρ ας	χεῖρ α		χεῖρ ας
5	ἄνερ	man	hand		

Base ending in μ or ν:

ὁ	κανών	κανόν ες
	κανόν ος	κανόν ων
	κανόν ι	κανό σι
	κανόν α	κανόν ας
	standard, rule	

3d plural consonant combinations:

$$\rho + \sigma\iota = \rho\alpha\sigma\iota \text{ or } \rho\sigma\iota$$
$$\nu + \sigma\iota = \sigma\iota$$
$$\gamma, \kappa, \chi + \sigma\iota = \xi\iota$$
$$\delta, \theta, \tau + \sigma\iota = \sigma\iota$$
$$\text{οντ} + \sigma\iota = \text{ουσι}$$

Base ending in γ, κ, or χ:

1	ἡ γυνή	γυναῖκ ες
2	γυναικ ός	γυναῖκ ῶν
3	γυναικ ί	γυναι ξί
4	γυναῖκ α	γυναῖκ ας
5	γύναι	woman

Base ending in δ:

1	ὁ παῖς	παῖδ ες
2	παῖδ ος	παῖδ ων
3	παιδ ί	παι σί
4	παῖδ α	παῖδ ας
5	boy, servant	

(THIRD DECLENSION NOUNS CONT.)

Base ending in θ or τ:

1	τὸ	πνεῦμα	πνεύματ α		ὁ	ἄρχων	ἄρχοντ ες
2		πνεύματ ος	πνευμάτ ων			ἄρχοντ ος	ἀρχόντ ων
3		πνεύματ ι	πνεύμα σι			ἄρχοντ ι	ἄρχου σι
4		πνεῦμα	πνεύματ α			ἄρχοντ α	ἄρχοντ ας
		spirit				ruler	

Base ending in a vowel: (Some endings show influence of the stem vowel.)

1	τὸ	ἔθνο ς	ἔθν η		ἡ	πόλι ς	πόλε ις		ὁ	ἰχθύ ς	ἰχθύ ες
2		ἔθνο υς	ἔθν ῶν			πόλε ως	πόλε ων			ἰχθύ ος	ἰχθύ ων
3		ἔθνε ι	ἔθνε σι			πόλε ι	πόλε σι			ἰχθύ ι	ἰχθύ σι
4		ἔθνο ς	ἔθν η			πόλι ν	πόλε ις			ἰχθύ ν	ἰχθύ ας
		nation				city				fish	

1	ὁ	βασιλεύ ς	βασιλε ῖς		ἡ	δέησι ς	δέήσε ις
2		βασιλέ ως	βασιλέ ων			δέησε ως	δέήσε ων
3		βασιλε ῖ	βασιλεῦ σι			δέησε ι	δέήσε σι
4		βασιλέ α	βασιλε ῖς			δέησι ν	δέησε ις
		king				prayer	

THIRD DECLENSION IRREGULARITIES:

It is apparent that several sets of endings are grouped under the third declension, since they show similarities. For some words it is easier to memorize their paradigms than to analyze the route of change that lies behind them. There may be no other word exactly formed by the same process.

1	ὁ	νοῦς	νοῖ		ὁ	βοῦς	βόες
2		νοῦ	νῶν			βοός	βοῶν
3		νῷ	νοῖς			βοΐ	βουσί
4		νοῦν	νοῦς			βοῦν	βόας/βοῦς
		mind				ox/bull; ἡ βοῦς cow

An Irregular *Adjective* That Builds With the Genitive Singular Base:

1	μέγας	μεγάλη	μέγα	μεγάλοι	μεγάλαι	μεγάλα
2	μεγάλου	μεγάλης	μεγάλου	μεγάλων	μεγάλων	μεγάλων
3	μεγάλῳ	μεγάλῃ	μεγάλῳ	μεγάλοις	μεγάλαις	μεγάλοις
4	μέγαν	μεγάλην	μέγα	μεγάλους	μεγάλας	μεγάλα
	great					

Only three consonants can be the final letter of *any Greek word*. These are **ν, ρ** and **ς**. [The only exception is the preposition ἐκ and its variation ἐξ.] Hence in the μέγας paradigm above the final λ of the gen. s. base μεγαλ changed to ς (nom. s.m.), was kept and followed by a vowel (nom. s.f.), and was dropped altogether (nom. s.n.).

THIRD DECLENSION ADJECTIVES:

Note that the feminine adjectives (columns 2 & 5) use the first declension.

	1	2	3	4	5	6
1	πᾶς	πᾶσ α	πᾶν	πάντ ες	πᾶσ αι	πάντ α
2	παντ ός	πάσ ης	παντ ός	πάντ ων	πασ ῶν	πάντ ων
3	παντ ί	πάσ ῃ	παντ ί	πᾶ σι	πᾶσ αις	πᾶ σι
4	πάντ α	πᾶσ αν	πᾶν	πάντ ας	πάσ ας	πάντ α

all, each, every

	1	2	3	4	5	6
1	πλατύ ς	πλατεῖ α	πλατ ύ	πλατε ῖς	πλατεῖ αι	πλατέ α
2	πλατέ ως	πλατεί ας	πλατέ ως	πλατέ ων	πλατει ῶν	πλατέ ων
3	πλατε ῖ	πλατεί ᾳ	πλατε ῖ	πλατέ σι	πλατεί εις	πλατέ σι
4	πλατύ ν	πλατεῖ αν	πλατ ύ	πλατε ῖς	πλατεί ας	πλατέ α

wide, broad

(*THIRD DECLENSION ADJECTIVES CONT.*):

	masc./fem.	neut.	masc./fem.	neut.
1	μονογεν ής	μονογεν ές	μονογεν εῖς	μονογεν ῆ
2	μονογεν οῦς	μονογεν οῦς	μονογεν ῶν	μονογεν ῶν
3	μονογεν εῖ	μονογεν εῖ	μονογεν έσι	μονογεν έσι
4	μονογεν ῆ	μονογεν ές	μονογεν εῖς	μονογεν ῆ
5	μονογεν ές			

only, unique

CARDINAL NUMBERS ONE THROUGH FOUR DECLINED:

	masc.	fem.	neut.		masc./fem.	neut.	masc./fem.	neut.
1	εἷς	μία	ἕν	δύο	τρεῖς	τρία	τέσσαρες	τέσσαρα
2	ἑνός	μιᾶς	ἑνός	δύο	τριῶν	τριῶν	τεσσάρων	τεσσάρων
3	ἑνί	μιᾷ	ἑνί	δυσί	τρισί	τρισί	τέσσαρσι	τέσσαρσι
4	ἕνα	μίαν	ἕν	δύο	τρεῖς	τρία	τέσσαρας	τέσσαρα
	one			two	three		four	

None of the cardinals 5–199 is declined until διακόσιοι = 200.

Useful Grammars for Exegesis

The heavy grammars listed here have scriptural indices that are the key to their usefulness for exegesis. Timothy Owings correlated the scriptural indices of eleven grammars, including all but one of those listed below, in a work entitled *A Cumulative Index to New Testament Greek Grammars*, Baker, 1983.

The grammars cited in this *Enchiridion* are referred to by author and initial capitals of the title. They are listed here according to my preference of their value for exegesis. Other arrangements would be possible were one to evaluate them for some other purpose.

The four-volume set published by T. and T. Clark of Edinburgh:
Moulton, James Hope. *A Grammar of NT Greek*:
    I. *Prolegomena*. 3d ed., 1978
    II. *Accidence and Word Formation*, 1979 [coauthor: W. F. Howard]
    III. *Syntax*, 1963 [coauthor: Nigel Turner]
    IV. *Style*, 1976 [exclusive author: Nigel Turner]
Robertson, A.T. *A Grammar of the Greek NT in the Light of Historical Research*. 4th ed. Nashville: Broadman, 1923.
Zerwick, Maximillian. *Biblical Greek*. Ed. and trans., Joseph Smith. Rome: Pontifical Biblical Institute, 1963.
Moule, C.F.D. *An Idiom Book of NT Greek*. Cambridge University Press, 2d ed., 1959.
Burton, E. de Witt. *Syntax of the Moods and Tenses in NT Greek*. Edinburgh: T. and T. Clark, 3d ed., 1898, reprint 1973.
Blass, F. and Debrunner, A. *A Grammar of the NT and Other Early Christian Literature*. Trans., Robert W. Funk. Chicago: University of Chicago, 1961.

DECLENSIONAL INFLECTIONS

FOR

PARSING NOUNS, PRONOUNS, AND ADJECTIVES

These charts are designed as visual software to enable you to identify from a word's ending its syntactical relationship—its case.

		First Declension				Second Dec.		Third Dec. (most, not all forms)							
Nominative	s.	α	η	ας	ης	ος	ον	ων	ες	η	ς	ος	ευς	ις	α
	pl.	αι	αι			οι	α	ες	α				εις	εις	ατα
Gen./Abl.	s.	ας	ης	ου		ου		ος	ων	ους	ος	ατος	εως		
	pl.	ων	ων			ων		ων	εων			ατων			
Dat./Inst./Loc.	s.	ᾳ	η			ῳ		ι	εσι	ι	ι	ατι			
	pl.	αις	αις			οις		[ου]σι	εσι	ευσι	ισι				
Accusative	s.	αν	ην			ον	ον	α	ας	εα	ιν	ατα			
	pl.	ας	ας			ους	α	ας	εις			ατα			
Vocative	s.	α				ε		ι	ες	αι	ευ				
	pl.	identical to the Nominative pl. in all declensions													

ALPHABETICAL ANALYSIS OF INFLECTIONS

α	nom s, pl, acc s, pl, voc s
ᾳ	d-i-l s
αι	nom pl, voc s
αν	acc s
ας	nom s, g-a s, acc pl
ασι	d-i-l pl
ατα	nom pl, acc pl
ατι	d-i-l s
ατος	g-a s
ατων	g-a pl
ε	voc s
εα	acc s
ει	d-i-l s
εις	nom pl, acc pl
ες	nom pl
εσι	d-i-l pl
εῦ	voc s
ευς	nom s
ευσι	d-i-l pl
εῶν	g-a pl
έως	g-a s
η	nom s, pl, acc pl
ῃ	d-i-l s
ης	nom s, g-a s
ι	d-i-l s
ιν	acc s
ις	nom s
οι	nom pl
οις	d-i-l pl
ο	nom s, acc s
ος	nom s, g-a s, acc s
ου	g-a s
ους	g-a s, acc pl
[ου]σι	d-i-l pl
ῳ	d-i-l s
ων	nom s, g-a pl

g-a = genitive or ablative
d-i-l = dative or instrumental or locative
Note: Any nom. pl. listed here could also be a voc. pl.

CASE DISTINCTIONS

All grammarians agree that the case of a word that can be declined provides—by its ending—an indication of the relation of that word to the sentence in which it occurs. Some grammarians abstract five cases and some eight. The former method stresses the *form* of a word and the latter the *general function* of a word, but neither method of counting cases can exist without depending to some degree on the other element, whether it be function or form. At the level of practical exegesis which method of case analysis one employs has less than critical importance. This is so since a further distinction—the *precise use* of the case—is also abstracted to specify one's understanding of the writer's intention in a particular word.

The Basic Ideas of the Case Appellations:

Nominative:	subject/specific designation
Genitive:	description/identification/attribution
Ablative:	separation/source
Dative:	personal interest
Instrumental:	means
Locative:	location
Accusative:	extension/termination
Vocative:	direct address

In the case usages that follow for the Ablative, Instrumental, and Locative, these identifications will be given on the left heading *and the comparable five-case designations will be given on the same line to the right.*

THE VOCATIVE CASE

Basic Idea: Direct Address

The one addressed is being 'called' [from the Latin past participle *vocatus*]. *Direct Address* is the only use of the vocative, but both nominative and vocative forms are used.

πάτερ ᾽Αβραάμ, ἐλέησόν με (Luke 16:24);   **ἡ παῖς**, ἔγειρε (Luke 8:54)

ἄγγελον τοῦ θεοῦ . . . εἰπόντα . . . **Κορνήλιε**. (Acts 10:3)

τί γὰρ οἶδας, **γύναι**, εἰ τὸν ἄνδρα σώσεις; (1 Cor. 7:16)

Σὺ δέ, ὦ **ἄνθρωπε** θεοῦ, ταῦτα φεῦγε (1 Tim. 6:11)

There are no vocative plural forms; the nominative plural is used instead. Nor are there any vocative forms for neuter nouns.

῎Ανδρες ἀδελφοὶ καὶ **πατέρες**, ἀκούσατε μου . . . ἀπολογίας (Acts 22:1)

THE NOMINATIVE CASE

Basic Idea: Specific Designation

Since in Greek the verb of the sentence always includes its own subject (at least as far as person and number), the noun in the nominative is appositional to the verb in naming the subject.

Uses within the Nominative Case:

1. *The Subject Nominative* designates the subject.

   καὶ ἡ ζωὴ ἐφανερώθη (1 John 1:2)

2. *The Predicate Nominative* demarcates the less definite of two nominatives linked by an equative (copulative) verb such as: εἰμί, γίνομαι, or ὑπάρχω. (The other, more definite nominative, is the subject nominative.)

   Ascertain the Predicate Nominative by comparing the two nominatives:

   (1) The predicate nominative will be the one *without the article* in most—not all—instances.

   ὥστε **κύριός** ἐστιν ὁ υἱὸς τοῦ ἀνθρώπου καὶ τοῦ σαββάτου (Mark 2:28)

   ὁ λόγος **σὰρξ** ἐγένετο (John 1:14)

   (2) The predicate nominative will be *the one that is not anaphoric.* (The nominative that continues the mention made [of it] in the immediately preceding context is anaphoric, and therefore it is the subject nominative of

the new clause.) *A pronoun is characteristically anaphoric and will always be the subject when used with an equative verb.*

ἐκ . . . πέτρας, ἡ πέτρα δὲ ἦν ὁ **Χριστός** (1 Cor. 10:4)

. . . τοῦ Χριστοῦ. Αὐτὸς γάρ ἐστιν ἡ **εἰρήνη** ἡμῶν (Eph. 2:13–14)

[The pronoun, Αὐτός, refers to Christ and serves as the subject, causing ἡ εἰρήνη—even though it is articular—to become the predicate nominative.]

ἐκήρυσσεν τὸν Ἰησοῦν ὅτι οὗτός ἐστιν ὁ **υἱὸς** τοῦ θεοῦ (Acts 9:20)

(3) The predicate nominative will be the *adjective* whenever one of the two nominatives is an adjective, whether articular or anarthrous.

τὸ φρέαρ ἐστὶν **βαθύ** [nom. s. neut.] (John 4:11)

Ἦν τὸ φῶς τὸ **ἀληθινόν** (John 1:9)

3. *Nominative of Apposition* restates, identifies, or complements the subject with which it occurs.

καθὼς εἶπεν Ἡσαΐας ὁ **προφήτης** (John 1:23)

ἀσπάζεται ὑμᾶς Λουκᾶς ὁ ἰατρὸς ὁ **ἀγαπητός** (Col. 4:14)

4. *Independent or Absolute Nominative* stands alone grammatically as a nominative either as the expectation of its context, or in spite of its context.

(1) As a picture hung on the wall, about which an assertion is possible:

ἴδε ὁ **ἀμνὸς** τοῦ θεοῦ ὁ αἴρων τὴν ἁμαρτίαν τοῦ κόσμου (John 1:29)

[The nom. rather than the acc. (as object of ἴδε) occurs here.]

῾Ο **νικῶν** δώσω αὐτῷ καθίσαι μετ᾽ ἐμοῦ ἐν τῷ θρόνῳ μου (Rev. 3:21)

(2) As the free-standing form for names and titles:

ὄνομα αὐτῷ **Ἰωάννης** (John 1:6)

ὑμεῖς φωνεῖτέ με· ὁ **διδάσκαλος**, καὶ ὁ **κύριος** (John 13:13)

Παῦλος καὶ **Τιμόθεος** δοῦλοι Χριστοῦ Ἰησοῦ πᾶσιν τοῖς ἁγίοις (Phil. 1:1)
[The bold nominatives tell who wrote the letter.]

ὁ οἶκός μου **οἶκος** προσευχῆς κληθήσεται (Matt. 21:13)

(3) As the customary case of exclamations:

λέγετε **εὐδία** ["fair weather!"], πυρράζει γὰρ ὁ οὐρανός (Matt. 16:2)

Ὦ **βάθος** πλούτου καὶ σοφίας καὶ γνώσεως θεοῦ (Rom. 11:33)

(4) As the anomalous transcender of grammatical regularities,

—resisting conformity to the noun with which it is in apposition:

ἀπὸ Ἰησοῦ Χριστοῦ, ὁ **μάρτυς**, ὁ **πιστός**, ὁ **πρωτότοκος** τῶν νεκρῶν καὶ ὁ **ἄρχων** τῶν βασιλέων τῆς γῆς (Rev. 1:5)

—resisting the influence of a preposition that takes another case:

εἰρήνη ἀπὸ **ὁ ὢν καὶ ὁ ἦν καὶ ὁ ἐρχόμενος** (Rev. 1:4)

[Note the next phrase that does conform to the grammar of the preposition:

καὶ ἀπὸ τῶν ἑπτὰ πνευμάτων . . . (Rev. 1:4).]

—resisting the case (acc. of specification) expected when telling how much:

ἐξήρχοντο **εἷς καθ᾽ εἷς** [instead of ἕνα with κατά] (John 8:9)

THE GENITIVE CASE

Basic Idea: Description/Identification/Attribution

Characteristic translational word: "of"

The Genitive Case qualifies or specifies an idea as to its identity or characteristics. Its root meaning is attribution—either of essential relationship or quality.

1. *Adjectival Genitive* asserts attributively a relationship between a genitive noun or pronoun and the noun it modifies. Also called *Genitive of Description,* this is the characteristic, adnominal genitive use.

   καὶ ἑρπετὰ τῆς γῆς (Acts 10:12)

2. *Possessive Genitive* identifies an owner:

   ἐν τῷ σώματι ὑμῶν (1 Cor. 6:20)

3. *Subjective Genitive.* The noun in the genitive produces the action (or is the "subject" of the action) *implied in the noun it modifies.*

   ὄψεται πᾶσα σὰρξ τὸ σωτήριον τοῦ **θεοῦ** (Luke 3:6)

4. *Objective Genitive.* The noun in the genitive receives the action (or is the "object" of the verb) *implied in the noun it modifies.*

   τὴν ἀποκάλυψιν τῶν **υἱῶν** τοῦ θεοῦ (Rom. 8:19)

   αὐξανόμενοι τῇ ἐπιγνώσει τοῦ **θεοῦ** (Col. 1:10)

5. *Genitive of Apposition* defines by equation; also called *Epexegetic Genitive*.

    θεός, ὁ δοὺς ἡμῖν τὸν ἀρραβῶνα τοῦ **πνεύματος** (2 Cor. 5:5)

6. *Adverbial Genitive of Time* identifies a temporal occasion, telling "when."

    οὗτος ἦλθεν πρὸς αὐτὸν **νυκτός** (John 3:2)

7. *Adverbial Genitive of Reference* qualifies an adjective "with reference to" that noun in the genitive.

    ἀνόμοις ὡς ἄνομος, μὴ ὢν ἄνομος **θεοῦ** ἀλλ' ἔννομος **Χριστοῦ** (1 Cor. 9:21)

    It may also key upon an adjective hidden in a verb, as "worthy" in καταξιόω ('consider worthy').

    καταξιωθῆναι ὑμᾶς τῆς **βασιλείας** τοῦ θεοῦ (2 Thess. 1:5)

8. *Adverbial Genitive of Purpose* tells "why."

    ἰδοὺ ἐξῆλθεν ὁ σπείρων **τοῦ σπείρειν** (Matt. 13:3)

    οἱ δὲ τὰ φαῦλα πράξαντες εἰς ἀνάστασιν **κρίσεως** (John 5:29)

9. *Genitive of Content* depicts (usually what fills) the interior of something or someone.

    γεμίσατε τὰς ὑδρίας **ὕδατος** (John 2:7)

    ἰδόντες δὲ οἱ Ἰουδαῖοι τοὺς ὄχλους ἐπλήσθησαν **ζήλου** (Acts 13:45)

10. *Genitive of Apparent Object.* Certain verbs have what seems to be their objects in the genitive instead of the accusative case. This construction happens because they have a built-in "of" or genitival, descriptive or identifying element in their idiomatic structure. Such are the following verbs:

(1) *Of Sensation* (e.g., hear of, taste of, lay hold of: ἀκούω, γεύομαι, ἐπιλαμβάνομαι, ἅπτω):

ἐάν τίς μου ἀκούσῃ τῶν **ῥημάτων** (John 12:47)

γευσαμένους τε τῆς **δωρεᾶς** τῆς ἐπουρανίου (Heb. 6:4)

ἐπιλαβοῦ τῆς αἰωνίου **ζωῆς** (1 Tim. 6:12)

(2) *Of Desiring or Aspiring* (ἐπιθυμέω, ὀρέγομαι):

Εἴ τις **ἐπισκοπῆς** ὀρέγεται (1 Tim. 3:1)

(3) *Of Sharing or Partaking* (μετέχω, μεταλαμβάνω)

Εἰ ἄλλοι τῆς ὑμῶν **ἐξουσίας** μετέχουσιν (1 Cor. 9:12)

(4) *Of Memory* (μνημονεύω, μιμνῄσκομαι):

μνημονεύετε τῆς **γυναικὸς** Λώτ (Luke 17:32)

(5) *Of Taking Charge Of, Ruling Over* (ἄρχω, κυριεύω, κατισχύω):

ἵνα καὶ **νεκρῶν** καὶ ζώντων κυριεύσῃ (Rom. 14:9)

(6) *Of Accusing or Treating with Contempt* (κατηγορέω):

καὶ κατηγόρουν **αὐτοῦ** οἱ ἀρχιερεῖς πολλά (Mark 15:3)

(7) *Of Bearing with or Neglecting* (ἀνέχω, ἀμελέω):

ἀνεχόμενοι **ἀλλήλων** ἐν ἀγάπῃ (Eph. 4:2)

11. *Genitive Absolute* consists of a noun or pronoun in the genitive and a participle in the genitive connected to the rest of the sentence adverbially. (If the participle takes an object, that object will be in the accusative case.)

καὶ **καθίσαντος αὐτοῦ** προσῆλθον αὐτῷ οἱ μαθηταί (Matt. 5:1)

ὁ λαὸς γὰρ ἅπας ἐξεκρέματο **αὐτοῦ ἀκούων** (Luke 19:48)

ἔτι **ἁμαρτωλῶν ὄντων ἡμῶν** Χριστὸς ὑπὲρ ἡμῶν ἀπέθανεν (Rom. 5:8)

σοῦ δὲ **ποιοῦντος** ἐλεημοσύνην, μὴ γνώτω ἡ ἀριστερά σου τί ποιεῖ ἡ δεξιά σου (Matt. 6:3)

12. *Prepositional Genitive.* A number of prepositions take their objects in the genitive, telling where, in what manner, for whose benefit, etc. This use, were it not for the prepositions, could be subsumed under the *Adverbial Genitive.* Such prepositions that will occur with the genitive are:

ἐπί, μετά, περί, ἀμφί, διά, ὑπέρ, κατά [73 times, ΝΤ].

καθήσεσθε ἐπὶ **θρόνων** (Luke 22:30)

82

THE ABLATIVE CASE

Basic Idea: Separation

(Latin: *ablativus*—that which is removed by separation)

Characteristic translational word: "from"

1. *Ablative of Separation:*   *Genitive of Separation*

   This basic ablative indicates either a physical or logical removal or distance.

   ξένοι τῶν **διαθηκῶν** (Eph. 2:12)

   γύναι, ἀπολέλυσαι τῆς **ἀσθενείας** σου (Luke 13:12)

2. *Ablative of Source:*   *Genitive of Source*

   The origination of something is traced back to that from which it came.

   τὴν ἐπαγγελίαν τοῦ **πατρός** ἣν ἠκούσατέ **μου** (Acts 1:4)

3. *Ablative of Comparison:*   *Genitive of Comparison*

   This use states that from which there was a separation in an unequal comparison. When translating into English this construction requires "than" instead of "from."

   μείζω **τούτων** ὄψῃ (John 1:50)

   πόσῳ οὖν διαφέρει ἄνθρωπος **προβάτου** (Matt. 12:12)

4. *Ablative of the Whole:* *Paritive Genitive*

   The word in the ablative indicates that from which a part has been taken.

   τὰ πρόβατα τὰ ἀπολωλότα **οἴκου** Ἰσραήλ (Matt. 15:24)

5. *Prepositional Ablative:* *Genitive of Agent*

   Certain prepositions take their objects in the ablative. Thus the "use" of the case is implicit in the meaning of the preposition.

   The prepositions of the ablative are predominately ἐκ, ἀπό, χωρίς, ὑπό, and παρά:

   'from' what/whom: ἀπὸ τῆς **συναγωγῆς** (Luke 4:38) [separation];

   'apart from' what/whom: χωρὶς **νόμου** (Rom. 3:21) [separation];

   'out of' what/whom: ἐκ θελήματος **σαρκὸς** (John 1:13) [source];

   'by means of' what/whom: μαρτυρουμένη ὑπὸ τοῦ **νόμου** (Rom. 3:21) [means imply logical separation];

   'of' what/whom: ἐξ **ὧν** οἱ πλείονες μένουσιν (1 Cor. 15:6) [separation from the whole];

   'by' what/whom: παρὰ **κυρίου** ἐγένετο αὕτη (Mark 12:11) [source].

THE DATIVE CASE

Basic Idea: Personal Interest

Characteristic translational words: "to," "for"

1. *Dative of Indirect Object* indicates the indirect recipient of the action of a transitive verb.

   οἴδατε δόματα ἀγαθὰ διδόναι τοῖς **τέκνοις ὑμῶν** (Luke 11:13)

2. *Dative of Advantage* shows "for" whose benefit something exists or is done.

   τὸ δὲ σῶμα οὐ τῇ **πορνείᾳ** ἀλλὰ τῷ **κυρίῳ** (1 Cor. 6:13)

   ἑαυτοῖς ποιήσατε φίλους (Luke 16:9)

3. *Dative of Disadvantage* shows to whose detriment something exists. Supply the word "against" whenever suitable.

   ὥστε μαρτυρεῖτε **ἑαυτοῖς** (Matt. 23:31)

4. *Possessive Dative* reveals to whom some one/thing belongs; this approximates a special dative of advantage.

   εἰσὶν **ἡμῖν** ἄνδρες τέσσαρες (Acts 21:23)

5. *Dative of Reference* indicates the person or personified idea to which the action of an *intransitive* verb refers.

ἤρξατο αὐτοῖς λέγειν τὰ μέλλοντα **αὐτῷ** συμβαίνειν (Mark 10:32)

οὐκ ἐψεύσω [2p.s aor. mid.] **ἀνθρώποις** ἀλλὰ τῷ **θεῷ** (Acts 5:4)

6. *Dative of Apparent Object.* Though the accusative case is the case of the direct object, certain verbs are internally constructed with personal implications so as to require their objects to be in the dative case.

ὁ δὲ ἀπειθῶν τῷ **υἱῷ** οὐκ ὄψεται ζωήν (John 3:36)

λατρεύειν **αὐτῷ** (Luke 1:74)

οἱ δὲ ἐν σαρκὶ ὄντες **θεῷ** ἀρέσαι οὐ δύνανται (Rom. 8:8)

καὶ ἐπετίμησεν **αὐτῷ** ὁ Ἰησοῦς λέγων (Luke 4:35)

οἱ δὲ εὐθέως ἀφέντες τὰ δίκτυα ἠκολούθησαν **αὐτῷ** (Matt. 4:20)

THE INSTRUMENTAL CASE

Basic Idea: Means

Characteristic translational words: "by" or "with," and sometimes "—ly"

1. *Instrumental of Means:*   *Instrumental Daive*

   This use tells that cause by which an effect is produced.

   χάριτί ἐστε σεσφσμένοι (Eph. 2:5)

2. *Instrumental Agent:*   *Dative Agent*

   This use tells the person by whom an effect is produced.

   ὅσοι γάρ **πνεύματι** θεοῦ ἄγονται (Rom. 8:14)

   Note: There are three ways to express *agency:*

      (1) Instrumental Agent (as exampled here) = by   (1) Dative Agent (by)

      (2) διά + genitive = "through" someone/thing   (2) διά + gen. (through)

      (3) ὑπό + ablative = "by" someone/thing   (3) ὑπό + gen. (by)

3. *Instrumental of Manner:*   *Dative of Manner*

   This adverbial use expresses *how* something is done.

   διδάξαι ὑμᾶς **δημοσίᾳ** ['publicly'] καὶ κατ᾽ οἴκους (Acts 20:20)

4. *Cognate Emphatic Instrumental:*   *Cognate Emphatic Daive*

   This use repeats the verb's idea in the cognate noun; the effect is emphatic. Such a construct reproduces a Hebrew idiom.

   ἐπιθυμίᾳ ἐπεθύμησα (Luke 22:15); **χαρᾷ** χαίρει (John 3:29)

THE LOCATIVE CASE

Basic Idea: Location

Characteristic translational word: "in"

1. *Locative of Place* designates spatial location.   *Locative Dative*

   καὶ ἔγνω τῷ **σώματι** ὅτι ἴαται (Mark 5:29)

2. *Locative of Time:*   *Dative of Time*

   This use locates the action *at* or *during* a period(s) of time. [*General time is expressed by the genitive, and duration of time by the accusative case.*]

   εἰ τοῖς **σάββασιν** θεραπεύσει αὐτόν (Mark 3:2)

3. *Locative of Sphere* indicates an abstract realm.   *Locative Dative*

   ψαλῶ τῷ **πνεύματι**, ψαλῶ δὲ καὶ τῷ **νοῖ** (1 Cor. 14:15)

4. *Locative Absolute:*   *Dative Absolute*

   A noun/pronoun in this case together with a participle in the same case is connected with the rest of the sentence adverbially. This use is rare in the NT: Luke 8:27

5. *Prepositional Locative:*   *Prepositional Dative*

   The preposition ἐν whenever it means "in" rather than "by" takes this case: ἐν πάσῃ **σοφίᾳ** καὶ φρονήσει (Eph. 1:8)

THE ACCUSATIVE CASE

Basic Idea: Extension/Termination

Characteristic translational words: none

1. *Accusative of Direct Object* indicates who/what is acted upon by a transitive verb, participle, or infinitive.

ὁ πατὴρ ἀγαπᾷ τὸν υἱόν (John 3:35)

ὁ θεὸς . . . ὁ εὐλογήσας ἡμᾶς ἐν . . . Χριστῷ (Eph. 1:3)

οἴδατε δόματα ἀγαθὰ διδόναι τοῖς τέκνοις ὑμῶν (Matt. 7:11)

2. *Accusative of Double Direct Object:*

Certain verbs such as those of teaching, asking, reminding, and dressing can take both a personal and an impersonal direct object, neither of which is an object complement. (The personal object acts like an indirect object logically but not literally.)

ἐδίδασκεν αὐτοὺς ἐν παραβολαῖς πολλά (Mark 4:2)

τὸν πατέρα αἰτήσει ὁ υἱὸς ἰχθύν (Luke 11:11)

ἐρωτήσω ὑμᾶς κἀγὼ λόγον ἕνα (Matt. 21:24)

ἐκεῖνος . . . ὑπομνήσει ὑμᾶς πάντα ἃ εἶπον ὑμῖν [ἐγώ] (John 14:26)

ἐξέδυσαν αὐτὸν τὴν πορφύραν καὶ ἐνέδυσαν αὐτὸν τὰ ἱμάτια αὐτοῦ (Mark 15:20)

3. *Accusative of General Reference* extends the basic verbal activity "with reference to" or "toward" some terminal other than a direct object.

αὐξήσωμεν εἰς αὐτὸν τὰ **πάντα** (Eph. 4:15)

μὴ ὀμνύετε, μήτε τὸν **οὐρανὸν** μήτε τὴν **γῆν** (James 5:12)

The accusative of General Reference occurs regularly with oaths:

ὁρκίζω ὑμᾶς τὸν **Ἰησοῦν** ὃν Παῦλος κηρύσσει (Acts 19:13)

The accusative of General Reference *occurs frequently with infinitives in which the extension is in the direction of affording a 'subject' for the verbal idea of the infinitive. The infinitive usually is in an objective status as regards the main verb of the sentence. For more examples see page 53.*

ὁ ὄχλος . . . ἤκουσαν τοῦτο **αὐτὸν** πεποιηκέναι τὸ σημεῖον (John 12:18)

ὁ δὲ θεὸς ἃ προκατήγγειλεν . . . παθεῖν τὸν **χριστὸν** αὐτοῦ, ἐπλήρωσεν οὕτως (Acts 3:18)

The Accusative of General Reference *also occurs with participles, in which the accusative word functions as the agent or 'subject' of the verbal action in the participle.*

τὸ δαιμόνιον . . . ἐξῆλθεν ἀπ᾽ αὐτοῦ **μηδὲν** βλάψαν αὐτὸν (Luke 4:35) [βλάπτω = harm]

καὶ **αὐτοὺς** ἐν τῷ πλοίῳ καταρτίζοντας τὰ δίκτυα (Mark 1:19)

4. *Cognate Accusative* consists of an object derived from the verb it completes, emphasizing in a secondary way and Hebraically what is already set forth in the verb itself. The cognate object may also have with it an adjective that is not cognate.

ἀγωνίζου τὸν καλὸν **ἀγῶνα** τῆς πίστεως (1 Tim. 6:12)

5. *Complementary Accusative* serves as an objective complement explaining or completing the objects of verbs of making, naming, taking to be, and proving to be.

ἐποίησεν τὸ ὕδωρ **οἶνον** (John 4:46)

Δαυὶδ οὖν **κύριον** αὐτὸν καλεῖ (Luke 20:44)

μὴ φοβηθῇς παραλαβεῖν Μαρίαν [εἶναι] τὴν **γυναῖκά** σου (Matt. 1:20)

ἐν ᾧ ὑμᾶς τὸ πνεῦμα τὸ ἅγιον ἔθετο **ἐπισκόπους** (Acts 20:28)

εἰ γὰρ ἃ κατέλυσα ταῦτα πάλιν οἰκοδομῶ, **παραβάτην** ἐμαυτὸν συνιστάνω (Gal. 2:18)

6. *Adverbial Accusative.*

In certain nouns the accusative case virtually becomes an adverb.

δωρεὰν ἐλάβετε, **δωρεὰν** δότε (Matt. 10:8)

Τὸ **λοιπόν**, ἀδελφοί μου, χαίρετε ἐν κυρίῳ (Phil. 3:1)

τὸν υἱόν ... ἀναβαίνοντα ὅπου ἦν τὸ **πρότερον** (John 6:62)

7. *Accusative of Extent of Time* indicates a temporal duration.

τί ὧδε ἑστήκατε **ὅλην τὴν ἡμέραν** ἀργοί; (Matt. 20:6)

ἰδοὺ **τοσαῦτα ἔτη** δουλεύω σοι (Luke 15:29)

8. *Accusative of Specification* tells how many (items, individuals) or how much (space), or where something is located.

ἀνέπεσαν οὖν οἱ ἄνδρες τὸν **ἀριθμὸν** ὡς πεντακισχίλιοι (John 6:10)

αὐτὸς ἀπεσπάσθη ἀπ᾽ αὐτῶν ὡσεὶ λίθου **βολὴν** (Luke 22:41)

γῇ Ζαβουλὼν καὶ γῇ Νεφθαλίμ, **ὁδὸν θαλάσσης**, πέραν τοῦ Ἰορδάνου (Matt. 4:15)

9. *Prepositional Accusative.*

Certain prepositions take the accusative. The chief of these are εἰς and ἀνά—used only with the accusative.

εἰς τὸν κόσμον [place to which] (John 1:9); ἀνὰ μέσον (1 Cor. 6:5)

The following prepositions occur with the accusative more than with the other cases:

πρὸς καιρὸν [extent of time] (Luke 8:13)

καθ᾽ ὅλην τὴν πόλιν [extent of space] (Luke 8:39)

ἐπὶ τὴν γῆν [place to which] (Matt. 15:35)

The following prepositions occur with the accusative, but not as much as with the genitive and ablative: διά, μετά, περί, ὑπέρ, and ὑπό.

διὰ τὴν χάριν [cause] (Rom. 15:15)

μετ᾽ οὐ πολλὰς ἡμέρας [extent of time] (Luke 15:13)

περὶ τὸν τόπον [extent of space] (Acts 28:7)

κεφαλὴν ὑπὲρ πάντα [extent of power] (Eph. 1:22)

ὑπὸ τὴν κραταιὰν χεῖρα τοῦ θεοῦ [place] (1 Peter 5:6)

CASE AND USE ANALYSIS ILLUSTRATED

Luke 8:26–29 Καὶ κατέπλευσαν εἰς τὴν χώραν[1] τῶν Γερασηνῶν,[2] ἥτις ἐστὶν ἀντιπέρα τῆς Γαλιλαίας.[3] ἐξελθόντι[4]

δὲ αὐτῷ[5] ἐπὶ τὴν γῆν[6] ὑπήντησεν ἀνήρ[7] τις[8] ἐκ τῆς πόλεως[9] ἔχων δαιμόνια[10] καὶ χρόνῳ[11] ἱκανῷ οὐκ ἐνεδύσατο

ἱμάτιον[12] καὶ ἐν οἰκίᾳ[13] οὐκ ἔμενεν ἀλλ᾽ ἐν τοῖς μνήμασιν.[14] ἰδὼν[15] δὲ τὸν Ἰησοῦν[16] ἀνακράξας[17] προσέπεσεν

αὐτῷ[18] καὶ φωνῇ[19] μεγάλῃ εἶπεν· τί[20] ἐμοὶ[21] καὶ σοί,[22] Ἰησοῦ[23] υἱὲ[24] τοῦ θεοῦ[25] τοῦ ὑψίστου;[26] δέομαί σου,[27] μή με[28]

βασανίσῃς. παρήγγειλεν γὰρ τῷ πνεύματι[29] τῷ ἀκαθάρτῳ[30] ἐξελθεῖν ἀπὸ τοῦ ἀνθρώπου.[31] πολλοῖς[32] γὰρ χρόνοις[33]

συνηρπάκει αὐτὸν[34] καὶ ἐδεσμεύετο ἁλύσεσιν[35] καὶ πέδαις[36] φυλασσόμενος καὶ διαρρήσσων τὰ δεσμὰ[37] ἠλαύνετο

ὑπὸ τοῦ δαιμονίου[38] εἰς τὰς ἐρήμους.[39]

The case abbreviation is followed by the use number assigned in this *Enchiridion:*

1. Ac-9	2. G-2	3. G-12	4. L-4	5. L-4	6. Ac-9	7. N-1	8. N-3
9. Ab-5	10. Ac-1	11. L-2	12. Ac-1	13. L-5	14. L-5	15. N-1	16. Ac-1
17. N-1	18. D-5	19. I-1	20. N-1	21. D-5	22. D-5	23. V	24. V
25. G-2	26. G-1	27. G-10(2)	28. Ac-1	29. D-6	30. D-6 appos.	31. Ab-5	32. L-2 appos.
33. L-2	34. Ac-1	35. I-1	36. I-1	37. Ac-1	38. Ab-5	39. Ac-9	

PRONOUN PARADIGMS

A pronoun is a representative word in relationship to its antecedent. Pronouns occur with great frequency in the NT. In the following inventory approximately 250 all-different pronoun forms are assembled within their respective categories.

PERSONAL PRONOUNS: (Inflectional forms, e.g., (1) = nominative, are numbered.)

First Person

(1) ἐγώ	I	ἡμεῖς	we
(2) ἐμοῦ, μου	my	ἡμῶν	our
(3) ἐμοί, μοι	to/for me	ἡμῖν	to/for us
(4) ἐμέ, με	me	ἡμᾶς	us

Second Person

(1) σύ	you	ὑμεῖς	you
(2) σοῦ, σου	your	ὑμῶν	your
(3) σοί, σοι	to/for you	ὑμῖν	to/for you
(4) σέ, σε	you	ὑμᾶς	you

Third Person

In the NT the *intensive* pronoun αὐτός, listed next, replaced the Attic third-person pronouns of classical Greek.

INTENSIVE PRONOUNS: (order: singular m. f. n., then plural m. f. n.)

(1)	αὐτός	αὐτή	αὐτό	αὐτοί	αὐταί	αὐτά
(2)	αὐτοῦ	αὐτῆς	αὐτοῦ	αὐτῶν	αὐτῶν	αὐτῶν
(3)	αὐτῷ	αὐτῇ	αὐτῷ	αὐτοῖς	αὐταῖς	αὐτοῖς
(4)	αὐτόν	αὐτήν	αὐτό	αὐτούς	αὐτάς	αὐτά

Translations and Uses of the Intensive Pronoun:

1. As the personal pronoun in the third person (he, his, to/for him, him, she, her, it, they, their, etc.)

   Εἶπεν δὲ πρὸς αὐτούς . . . He said to *them* . . . (Luke 24:44)

2. To emphasize a noun or pronoun with which it agrees (–self, even); it never comes between a noun and its definite article when it has this meaning.

   αὐτὸς Δαυιδ εἶπεν . . . David *himself* said . . . (Mark 12:36)

3. To identify a noun or pronoun with something already mentioned as being "the same." It comes *between* the noun and its definite article, or it may stand as a pronoun with the article alone.

   τὸ αὐτὸ πνεῦμα—the *same* spirit (2 Cor. 4:13)

   οἱ ἐθνικοὶ τὸ αὐτὸ ποιοῦσιν The nations do the *same*. (Matt. 5:47)

4. As a demonstrative (this, that, these, those)

   ἐν αὐτῇ τῇ ὥρᾳ in *that* hour (Luke 12:12)

POSSESSIVE PRONOUNS: (order: singular m. f. n., then plural m. f. n.)

		singular m.	f.	n.	plural m.	f.	n.	
1st Per. S.	(1)	ἐμός	ἐμή	ἐμόν	ἐμοί	ἐμαί	ἐμά	my
	(2)	ἐμοῦ	ἐμῆς	ἐμοῦ	ἐμῶν	ἐμῶν	ἐμῶν	
	(3)	ἐμῷ	ἐμῇ	ἐμῷ	ἐμοῖς	ἐμαῖς	ἐμοῖς	
	(4)	ἐμόν	ἐμήν	ἐμόν	ἐμούς	ἐμάς	ἐμά	
1st Per. Pl.	(1)	ἡμέτερος	ἡμετέρα	ἡμέτερον	ἡμέτεροι	ἡμέτεραι	ἡμέτερα	our
	(2)	ἡμετέρου	ἡμετέρας	ἡμετέρου	ἡμετέρων	ἡμετέρων	ἡμετέρων	
	(3)	ἡμετέρῳ	ἡμετέρᾳ	ἡμετέρῳ	ἡμετέροις	ἡμετέραις	ἡμετέροις	
	(4)	ἡμέτερον	ἡμετέραν	ἡμέτερον	ἡμετέρους	ἡμετέραις	ἡμέτερα	
2nd Per. S.	(1)	σός	σή	σόν	σοί	σαί	σά	your
	(2)	σοῦ	σῆς	σοῦ	σῶν	σῶν	σῶν	
	(3)	σῷ	σῇ	σῷ	σοῖς	σαῖς	σοῖς	
	(4)	σόν	σήν	σόν	σούς	σάς	σά	

2nd Per. Pl.						
(1)	ὑμέτερος	ὑμέτερα	ὑμέτερον	ὑμέτεροι	ὑμέτεραι	ὑμέτερα
(2)	ὑμετέρου	ὑμετέρας	ὑμετέρου	ὑμετέρων	ὑμετέρων	ὑμετέρων
(3)	ὑμετέρῳ	ὑμετέρᾳ	ὑμετέρῳ	ὑμετέροις	ὑμετέραις	ὑμετέροις
(4)	ὑμέτερον	ὑμετέραν	ὑμέτερον	ὑμετέρους	ὑμετέρας	ὑμέτερα

your

3rd Per. S/Pl.   (Gen.)   (Dat.) Second and third inflectional forms of αὐτός are used (his, her, its, their)

Possessive pronouns agree in gender and number with that *possessed*:

τὸν ἄνδρα σου [masc. sing. "your husband"] (John 4:16)

Possession is denoted in all the following ways:

1. By the use of possessive pronouns.

2. By the article when the context clearly indicates the possessor.

3. By the Possessive Genitive of the personal pronoun.

4. By the Possessive Genitive of the reflexive pronoun.

5. By the Possessive Dative of the personal pronoun.

6. By ἴδιος when the idea of possession is emphatic.

DEMONSTRATIVE PRONOUNS:

Immediate Demonstrative (this, these)

(1)	οὗτος	αὕτη	τοῦτο	οὗτοι	αὗται	ταῦτα
(2)	τούτου	ταύτης	τούτου	τούτων	τούτων	τούτων
(3)	τούτῳ	ταύτῃ	τούτῳ	τούτοις	ταύταις	τούτοις
(4)	τοῦτον	ταύτην	τοῦτο	τούτους	ταύτας	ταῦτα

Remote Demonstrative (that, those)

(1)	ἐκεῖνος	ἐκείνη	ἐκεῖνο	ἐκεῖνοι	ἐκεῖναι	ἐκεῖνα
(2)	ἐκείνου	ἐκείνης	ἐκείνου	ἐκείνων	ἐκείνων	ἐκείνων
(3)	ἐκείνῳ	ἐκείνῃ	ἐκείνῳ	ἐκείνοις	ἐκείναις	ἐκείνοις
(4)	ἐκεῖνον	ἐκείνην	ἐκεῖνο	ἐκείνους	ἐκείνας	ἐκεῖνα

Archaic Demonstratives (this-here one)

ὅδε   ἥδε   τόδε

INDEFINITE PRONOUNS:

The indefinite pronoun points out persons and things less clearly than demonstratives do. Characteristic translations are: someone, anyone, some, any, somebody, a certain one, anything, something. Τις is *enclitic* in all its forms, so this paradigm has been given just as if each one were surrounded by text and therefore without the accent expected on any word that stands alone. When the indefinite pronoun retains an accent as at the beginning of a sentence, the forms are accented like the interrogative pronouns.

(1) τις	τις	τι	τινες	τινες	τινα
(2) τινος	τινος	τινος	τινων	τινων	τινων
(3) τινι	τινι	τινι	τισι	τισι	τισι
(4) τινα	τινα	τι	τινας	τινας	τινα

INTERROGATIVE PRONOUNS:

Except for the difference in accent, the interrogative τίς is declined just like the indefinite τις. It may also serve as an Interrogative Adjective.

(1) τίς	τίς	τί	τίνες	τίνες	τίνα
(2) τίνος	τίνος	τίνος	τίνων	τίνων	τίνων
(3) τίνι	τίνι	τίνι	τίσι	τίσι	τίσι
(4) τίνα	τίνα	τί	τίνας	τίνας	τίνα

Qualitative Interrogative Pronouns: ποῖος, α, ον—what sort of?

Quantitative Interrogative Pronouns: πόσος, η, ον—how much/many?

RELATIVE PRONOUNS:

A relative pronoun connects a subordinate clause with a main clause and qualifies or refers to a substantive, called its antecedent. It must agree with its antecedent in *gender* and *number* but is free to determine its case according to its use in the clause in which it occurs. In some instances the case of the relative is attracted to correspond to that of its antecedent and sometimes vice versa. When the relative pronoun is used substantivally there may be no antecedent. Usually the relative clause is adjectival, however.

The *Relative* Pronoun

(who, which, that; he whom, that which; the one who, those that, etc.)

(1)	ὅς	ἥ	ὅ		οἵ	αἵ	ἅ
(2)	οὗ	ἧς	οὗ		ὧν	ὧν	ὧν
(3)	ᾧ	ᾗ	ᾧ		οἷς	αἷς	οἷς
(4)	ὅν	ἥν	ὅ		οὕς	ἅς	ἅ

The *Indefinite* Relative Pronoun

(whoever, every one who, such a one who)

(1)	ὅστις	ἥτις	ὅ τι		οἵτινες	αἵτινες	ἅτινα
(2)	ὅτου				——	——	——
(3)	——		ὅ τι		——	——	——
(4)	——		ὅ τι		——	——	——

The indefinite relative may act as a regular simple relative (Luke 2:4)

COORDINATION OF RELATIVE PRONOUNS

A relative pronoun begins a clause qualifying a (preceding) substantive. The relative pronoun's case will normally be determined by its function in the clause it introduces. As a pronoun it ordinarily has an antecedent—a word in the preceding context to which it refers and agrees in gender and number.

Normal Determination of Case: (ex. = nom. subj. of its clause)

ζητεῖτέ με ἀποκτεῖναι ἄνθρωπον **ὃς** τὴν ἀλήθειαν ὑμῖν λελάληκα (John 8:40)

Attraction of the Relative Pronoun to the Case of Its Antecedent (ex. = gen., not acc.)

περὶ πάντων **ὧν** ἐποίησεν (Luke 3:19)

Attraction of the Relative Pronoun Sometimes to the Gender of Its Predicate (not its Antecedent)

τὴν μάχαιραν τοῦ πνεύματος, **ὅ** ἐστιν ῥῆμα θεοῦ (Eph. 6:17)

Self-Containment of Relative Pronoun Without an Antecedent:

ἃ ἐγὼ ἑόρακα παρὰ τῷ πατρὶ λαλῶ (John 8:38, ἃ = 'the things that')

Quantitative Relative Pronouns

ὅσος, -η, -ον—as much, as far, as many, as great, as long

πόσος, -η, ον—how great, how much, how many

τοσοῦτος, -αύτη, -οῦτον—so great, so large, so far, so strong

Qualitative Relative Pronouns

οἷος, -α, -ον—of what sort, such as

ὁποῖος, οἵα, οἷον—of what sort

ποταπός, ἡ, όν—of what sort, of what kind

τοιοῦτος, -αύτη, -οῦτον—of such a kind, such

NEGATIVE PRONOUNS: (These are *always* singular.)—no one, nothing, etc.

(1)	μηδείς	μηδεμία	μηδέν	οὐδείς	οὐδεμία	οὐδέν
(2)	μηδενός	μηδεμιᾶς	μηδενός	οὐδενός	οὐδεμιᾶς	οὐδενός
(3)	μηδενί	μηδεμιᾷ	μηδενί	οὐδενί	οὐδεμιᾷ	οὐδενί
(4)	μηδένα	μηδεμίαν	μηδέν	οὐδένα	οὐδεμίαν	οὐδέν

REFLEXIVE PRONOUNS:

The action reflects back to the subject (of myself, to yourselves, himself, themselves, etc.) but does not occur in the nominative.

(2)	ἐμαυτοῦ	ἐμαυτῆς	(of myself)		
(3)	ἐμαυτῷ	ἐμαυτῇ	(for myself)		
(4)	ἐμαυτόν	ἐμαυτήν	(myself)		
(2)	σεαυτοῦ	σεαυτῆς	(of yourself)		
(3)	σεαυτῷ	σεαυτῇ	(for yourself)		
(4)	σεαυτόν	σεαυτήν	(yourself)		
(2)	ἑαυτοῦ	ἑαυτῆς	ἑαυτοῦ	(of himself)	
(3)	ἑαυτῷ	ἑαυτῇ	ἑαυτῷ	(for himself)	
(4)	ἑαυτόν	ἑαυτήν	ἑαυτό	(himself)	

(2)	ἑαυτῶν	ἑαυτῶν		(of ourselves)
(3)	ἑαυτοῖς	ἑαυταῖς		(for ourselves)
(4)	ἑαυτούς	ἑαυτάς		(ourselves)
(2)	ἑαυτῶν	ἑαυτῶν		(of yourselves)
(3)	ἑαυτοῖς	ἑαυταῖς		(for yourselves)
(4)	ἑαυτούς	ἑαυτάς		(yourselves)
(2)	ἑαυτῶν	ἑαυτῶν	ἑαυτῶν	(of themselves)
(3)	ἑαυτοῖς	ἑαυταῖς	ἑαυτοῖς	(for themselves)
(4)	ἑαυτούς	ἑαυτάς	ἑαυτά	(themselves)

RECIPROCAL PRONOUNS:

A plural subject interacts; hence the pronoun is only in the plural (one another, each other); it cannot be in the nominative.

	m.	f.	n.	
(2)	ἀλλήλων	ἀλλήλων	ἀλλήλων	(of one another)
(3)	ἀλλήλους	ἀλλήλαις	ἀλλήλοις	(to one another)
(4)	ἀλλήλους	ἀλλήλας	ἄλληλα	(one another)

Other ways to show reciprocity:

1. The use of the middle voice with a plural subject:

   ἐβουλεύσαντο δὲ οἱ ἀρχιερεῖς (John 12:10)

   Αἱ γυναῖκες, ὑποτάσσεσθε τοῖς ἀνδράσιν (Col. 3:18)

2. The use of a reflexive pronoun in the plural:

   λέγοντες πρὸς ἑαυτούς (Mark 10:26)

   εἰρηνεύετε ἐν ἑαυτοῖς (1 Thess. 5:13)

(Isa. 40:8) דְּבַר־אֱלֹהֵינוּ יָקוּם לְעוֹלָם

τὸ δὲ ῥῆμα κυρίου μένει εἰς τὸν αἰῶνα (1 Peter 1:25)

An excellent set of references for OT quotations and allusions—perhaps, the best to be found anywhere—are located in the margins of the Nestle-Aland text of the NT.

3
ADJECTIVES, ADVERBS, ARTICLES

ADJECTIVES

An adjective agrees in case, number, and gender with the substantive it modifies.
Greek adjectives occur in one of three degrees: (1) simple; (2) comparative; (3) superlative

SIMPLE ADJECTIVES:

πιστός, ή, όν = faithful, believing (m. f. n.)
ξένος, η, ον = strange, foreign (m. f. n.)

Third Declension Simple Adjectives

	m.s.	m.pl.	n.s.	n.pl.
(1)	σώφρων	σώφρονες	σῶφρον	σώφρονα
(2)	σώφρονος	σωφρόνων	σώφρονος	σωφρόνων
(3)	σώφρονι	σώφροσι	σώφρονι	σώφροσι
(4)	σώφρονα	σώφρονας	σῶφρον	σώφρονα

	m.s.	m.pl.	n.s.	n.pl.
(1)	ἀληθής	ἀληθεῖς	ἀληθές	ἀληθῆ
(2)	ἀληθοῦς	ἀληθῶν	ἀληθοῦς	ἀληθῶν
(3)	ἀληθεῖ	ἀληθέσι	ἀληθεῖ	ἀληθέσι
(4)	ἀληθῆ	ἀληθεῖς	ἀληθές	ἀληθῆ
(5)	ἀληθές	ἀληθεῖς		

	m.s.	m.pl.	f.s.	f.pl.	n.s.	n.pl.
(1)	εὐθύς	εὐθεῖς	εὐθεῖα	εὐθεῖαι	εὐθύ	εὐθέα
(2)	εὐθέος	εὐθέων	εὐθείας	εὐθειῶν	εὐθέος	εὐθέων
(3)	εὐθεῖ	εὐθέσι	εὐθείᾳ	εὐθείαις	εὐθεῖ	εὐθέσι
(4)	εὐθύν	εὐθεῖς	εὐθεῖαν	εὐθείας	εὐθύ	εὐθέα

σώφρων, ον = prudent
εὐθύς, εῖα, ύ = straight
ἀληθής, ές = true

COMPARATIVE AND SUPERLATIVE ADJECTIVES

COMPARATIVE ADJECTIVES:

The Greek comparative adjective is usually translated into English by "–er" or "more . . ."

ἰσχυρός, ά, όν = strong, mighty, powerful

ἰσχυρότερος, ἰσχυρότερα, ἰσχυρότερον nom. s. m. f. n. + s. noun } "stronger"
ἰσχυρότεροι ἰσχυρότεραι ἰσχυρότερα nom. pl. m. f. n. + pl. noun }

An adjective like σοφός, ή, όν (wise) lengthens the vowel before the ending.

σοφώτερος, σοφωτέρα, σοφώτερον nom. s. m. f. n. + s. noun = "wiser"

An adjective like ἄφρων, [ων], ον (foolish, ignorant) takes its stem from ἄφρονος—gen. s.

ἀφρονέστερος, ἀφρονεστέρα, ἀφρονέστερον nom. s. m. f. n + s. noun = "more ignorant"

An irregular adjective like μέγας, μεγάλη, μέγα (great) uses a third declension paradigm instead of the regular comparative endings. Contracted forms are in bold print.

m. f., s.		n. s.	m. f., pl.		n. pl.	
μείζων		μεῖζον	μείζονες	**μείζους**	μείζονα	**μείζω**
μείζονος		μείζονος	μειζόνων		μειζόνων	
μείζονι		μείζονι	μείζοσι		μείζουσι	
μείζονα	**μείζω**	μεῖζον	μείζονας	**μείζους**	μείζονα	**μείζω**
"greater" + s. noun			"greater" + pl. noun			

Comparative Constructions

1. The comparative adjective (in the ascriptive or restrictive position) plus a noun:

   κρείττονος ἐλπίδος δι᾽ ἧς ἐγγίζομεν τῷ θεῷ (Heb. 7:19)
   ἐκβληθήσονται εἰς τὸ σκότος τὸ ἐξώτερον (Matt. 8:12)

2. The comparative adjective used as a substantive:

   χωρὶς δὲ πάσης ἀντιλογίας τὸ ἔλαττον ὑπὸ τοῦ κρείττονος εὐλογεῖται (Heb. 7:7)

3. The simple or the comparative adjective plus the particle ἤ:

   καλόν σοί ἐστιν εἰσελθεῖν εἰς τὴν ζωὴν κυλλὸν ἢ χωλὸν ἢ δύο χεῖρας ἢ δύο πόδας ἔχοντα βληθῆναι εἰς τὸ πῦρ τὸ αἰώνιον (Matt. 18:8)

   [Often the use of the simple adjective plus ἤ for comparison has resulted from a Hebraism, since neither Hebrew nor Aramaic had a comparative form: λευκοὶ οἱ ὀδόντες αὐτοῦ ἢ γάλα (Gen. 49:12b).]

   κρεῖττον γάρ ἐστιν γαμῆσαι ἢ πυροῦσθαι (1 Cor. 7:9)

4. The comparative adjective + preposition followed by accusative case:

   ὅτι οἱ υἱοὶ τοῦ αἰῶνος τούτου φρονιμώτεροι ὑπὲρ τοὺς υἱοὺς τοῦ φωτὸς (Luke 16:8)
   τὸ δὲ ἐπιμένειν ἐν τῇ σαρκὶ ἀναγκαιότερον δι᾽ ὑμᾶς (Phil. 1:24)

5. The comparative adjective + the ablative [genitive] of comparison ("than"):

   ὁ δὲ ὀπίσω μου ἐρχόμενος ἰσχυρότερός μού ἐστιν (Matt. 3:11)

6. The comparative adjective is sometimes used for the rarer superlative:

   μικρότερον ὂν πάντων τῶν σπερμάτων τῶν ἐπὶ τῆς γῆς (Mark 4:31)

SUPERLATIVE ADJECTIVES:

The Greek superlative adjective is usually translated by "–est" or "most . . ."

ἰσχυρότατος, ἰσχυροτάτα, ἰσχυρότατον nom. s. m. f. n. with s. noun = "strongest"
ἰσχυρότατοι, ἰσχυρόταται, ἰσχυρότατα nom. pl. m., f., n. with pl. noun = "strongest"

An adjective like σοφός, ή, όν (wise) lengthens the vowel before the ending.
σοφώτατος, σοφωτάτα, σοφώτατον nom. s. m., f., n. with s. noun = "wisest"

An adjective like ἄφρων, [ων], ον (foolish, ignorant) takes its stem from ἄφρονος—gen. s.
ἀφρονέστατος, ἀφρονεστατα, ἀφρονέστατον nom. s. m., f., n. = "most foolish"

Important Irregular Superlatives:

μέγας, μεγάλη, μέγα (great); comparative = μείζων, ον (greater);
μέγιστος, μεγίστη, μέγιστον, μέγιστοι, μέγισται, μέγιστα = "greatest"

πολύς, πολλή, πολύ (many, much); comparative = πλείων, ον [or πλέων] (more);
πλεῖστος, πλείστη, πλεῖστον, πλεῖστοι, πλεῖσται, πλεῖστα = "most"

[ἀγαθός], comparative κρείττων, ον (better); superlative **κράτιστος, η, ον = "best"**
κράτιστε = voc. (Luke 1:3)
κρείσσων, ον

ADVERBS

COMPARATIVE AND SUPERLATIVE ADVERBS

Just as adverbs are regularly formed by replacing the corresponding adjectival ending of the second inflectional form plural (ων) with ως (e.g., καλῶν becomes καλῶς), in similar fashion does the regular -τερος of the comparative adjective become -τέρως in the comparative adverb: δεῖ **περισσοτέρως** προσέχειν ἡμᾶς τοῖς ἀκουσθεῖσιν (Heb. 2:1).

Also the comparative adverb is formed by using the *comparative adjective in the accusative singular neuter*:
αἵματι ῥαντισμοῦ **κρεῖττον** λαλοῦντι παρὰ τὸν Ἄβελ (Heb. 12:24)

The *superlative adverb* likewise uses the *accusative*, but in the *plural*, of the *neuter* gender of the superlative adjective.

ἵνα ὡς **τάχιστα** ἔλθωσιν (Acts 17:15)

COMPARATIVES AND SUPERLATIVES OF CERTAIN ADVERBS:

Simple	Comparative	Superlative
μάλα (very)	μᾶλλον (more, rather)	μάλιστα (most, especially)
πολλά, πολύ (greatly, very much)	πλεῖον (more)	
	πλέον (more)	
εὖ (adv.) well	κρεῖττον (better)	
	κρεῖσσον (better)	
	βέλτίον (better)	
ἡδέως gladly	ἥδιον (more gladly)	ἥδιστα (very gladly)
ἐγγύς near	ἐγγύτερον (nearer)	ἔγγιστα (nearest)
ταχύ quickly	ταχίον (more quickly)	τάχιστα (most quickly)
ταχέως, at once		

DISTINCTIVE CORRELATIVE ADVERBS:

	Time	Place	Manner
relative	ὅτε = when	οὗ = where	ὡς = as
specific	τότε = then	ὧδε = here	οὕτως = thus, in such a manner
		ἐκεῖ = there	
interrog.	πότε; = when?	ποῦ; = where?	πῶς; = how?
	πότε = when	ποῦ = where	πῶς = how (indirect question)
indef.	{ ποτέ = once	{ πού = somewhere	{ πώς = somehow
	{ ποτε = (enclitic form)	{ που = (enclitic form)	{ πως = (enclitic form)

THE ARTICLE

The Greek article is a linguistic *handle* for holding a word or group of words in thought. On average every seventh word is the article.

Absence of an Indefinite Article: "a, an"

No indefinite article exists in Greek. However, it should be supplied in English translation wherever it is needed to preserve the sense/style.

καὶ ἰδὼν συκῆν ἀπὸ μακρόθεν . . . (Mark 11:13)

When the Greek NT writers just had to have the equivalent of an indefinite article, they employed one of two means:

(1) They used the number "one": εἷς, μία, ἕν.

καὶ ἰδὼν συκῆν μίαν ἐπὶ τῆς ὁδοῦ . . . (Matt. 21:19)

(2) They used the indefinite pronoun: τὶς "a certain . . . ," "some."

ἄνθρωπός τις ἦν πλούσιος . . . (Luke 16:1)

The Definite Article: "the" (m., f., n., singular and plural)

(1)	ὁ	ἡ	τό	οἱ	αἱ	τά
(2)	τοῦ	τῆς	τοῦ	τῶν	τῶν	τῶν
(3)	τῷ	τῇ	τῷ	τοῖς	ταῖς	τοῖς
(4)	τόν	τήν	τό	τούς	τάς	τά

Articular Constructions:

Use of the Greek article indicates particularity. It points out or demonstrates less emphatically than the demonstratives (this/these; that/those) p. **99**. The article holds up for consideration as little as one letter or as much as a lengthy clause:

τὸ ὦ (Rev. 22:13)

. . . ἐν τῷ ἀγαπήσεις τὸν πλησίον σου ὡς σεαυτόν (Gal. 5:14)

The Versatility of the Greek Article:

While articles in English occur only before nouns, gerunds, adjectives, and adverbs, in Greek the article *also* may be used with:

pronouns   τῶν γὰρ τοιούτων ἐστιν ἡ βασιλεία τῶν οὐρανῶν (Matt. 19:14)

proper names   εἶπεν πρὸς τὸν Σίμωνα (Luke 5:4)

participles   οἱ γεγραμμένοι ἐν τῷ βιβλίῳ τῆς ζωῆς (Rev. 21:27)

infinitives   τοῦ μὴ ἐπιγνῶναι αὐτόν (Luke 24:16)

prepositional & other phrases   ἡ πίστις ὑμῶν ἡ πρὸς τὸν θεὸν (1 Thess. 1:8)

clauses, both short & long   τὸ τί ἂν θέλοι καλεῖσθαι αὐτό (Luke 1:62)

The Bracketing Force of the Article:

When the Greek article is used with more than one word, it "brackets" everything following it inclusive of the word(s) it modifies.

ἡ οἰκοῦσα ἐν ἐμοὶ ἁμαρτία = ἡ [οἰκοῦσα ἐν ἐμοὶ ἁμαρτία] (Rom. 7:17)
'the dwelling-in-me sin'

FUNCTIONS OF THE ARTICLE

1. *Featuring a particular word or group of words for syntactical relations:*

κηρύσσων τὸ εὐαγγέλιον (Matt. 9:35)

2. *Indication of previous mention (the anaphoric use):*

ἀπέστειλαν οἱ ἀρχιερεῖς . . . ὑπηρέτας . . .
῏Ηλθον οὖν **οἱ** ὑπηρέται πρὸς **τοὺς** ἀρχιερεῖς . . . (John 7:32, 45)

3. *Intensification of the demonstrative adjective/pronoun:*

Its position lies between the demonstrative and the noun modified.

οὗτος **ὁ** ἄνθρωπος . . . (Luke 14:30)

4. *Designation of a class, group, or a representative individual (generic use):*

αὐτὸς ἔδωκεν **τοὺς** μὲν ἀποστόλους, **τοὺς** δὲ προφήτας, **τοὺς** δὲ εὐαγγελιστάς (Eph. 4:11)
ἄξιος **ὁ** ἐργάτης τοῦ μισθοῦ αὐτοῦ (1 Tim. 5:18)

5. *Substitution for a possessive pronoun (as in French and German):*

οὐδεὶς ἐπέβαλεν ἐπ᾽ αὐτὸν **τὰς** χεῖρας (John 7:44)

6. *Substitution for a personal pronoun:*

λέγει αὐτοῖς· τί ζητεῖτε; **οἱ** δὲ εἶπαν αὐτῷ· ῥαββί . . . (John 1:38)

πάντες οἱ ἅγιοι, μάλιστα δὲ **οἱ** ἐκ τῆς Καίσαρος οἰκίας (Phil. 4:22)

οὐ μόνον **τὸ** τῆς συκῆς ποιήσετε, ἀλλὰ . . . (Matt. 21:21)

7. *Emphasis upon the accompanying adjective:*

(1) in the ascriptive attributive position—

καὶ **τὰ** ἴδια πρόβατα φωνεῖ (John 10:3)

(2) in the restrictive attributive position—

Ἐγώ εἰμι ὁ ποιμὴν **ὁ** καλός (John 10:11)

8. *Alternative to the vocative:*

ἐφώνησεν λέγων· **ἡ** παῖς, ἔγειρε (Luke 8:54)

9. *Concretion for abstractions:*

Ἐκζητήσατε **τὸ** καλὸν καὶ μὴ **τὸ** πονηρόν (Amos 5:14, LXX)

10. *Hendiadys* ('one through [joining] two'—ἕν + διά + δυσί [δύο]) or Granville Sharp's Rule:

Construction: *article* + noun + καί + noun = one unit

(Both nouns must be of the same gender and number.)

ὁ θεὸς καὶ πατὴρ = 'God the Father' or 'the God who is Father' (Eph. 1:3)

τοὺς δὲ ποιμένας καὶ διδασκάλους =   { "and pastor-teachers" (Eph. 4:11)
   "and shepherds who are teachers"

[This article is used here generically as well as forming the first word of the hendiadys.]

Additional nouns can be added in sequence: *hendiatrisin* (Matt. 17:1); *hendiatessarin* (Eph. 3:18).

Note: The unitizing of a hendiadys does not *absolutely* identify the two nouns as one, but functionally they coalesce:

τῷ θεμελίῳ τῶν ἀποστόλων καὶ προφητῶν (Eph. 2:20)

πρὸς τοὺς ἀποστόλους καὶ πρεσβυτέρους εἰς Ἰερουσαλὴμ (Acts 15:2)

μετέβη ἐκεῖθεν τοῦ διδάσκειν καὶ κηρύσσειν ἐν ταῖς πόλεσιν αὐτῶν (Matt. 11:1)

ANARTHROUS CONSTRUCTION

Anarthrous [*an* (not) + *athron* (joint, article)] means the absence of the article where it could have been used if another meaning were intended. The article is *not* found in the following instances:

1. When a personal word designates its denotation more than any specific application to an individual:

   παραδώσει ἀδελφὸς ἀδελφὸν εἰς θάνατον καὶ πατὴρ τέκνον (Mark 13:12)
   εἰ ἔξεστιν ἀνδρὶ γυναῖκα ἀπολῦσαι (Mark 10:2)

2. When a proper name, construed to be definite in itself, occurs:

   Θωμᾶς δὲ εἷς ἐκ τῶν δώδεκα (John 20:24)

   [But, of course, a proper name may have the article for emphasis or some contextual reason like anaphora.
   ἔρχεται ὁ ᾽Ιησοῦς (John 20:26)]

3. When used with a preposition a word is far less likely to have the article than when no preposition occurs.

   τοῦ κόσμου . . . ἐν κόσμῳ (Col. 2:20, 21)

4. When a predicate noun *precedes* an equative verb [εἰμί or γίνομαι]:

φῶς εἰμι τοῦ κόσμου (John 9:5)

Contrast: ἐγὼ εἰμι τὸ φῶς τοῦ κόσμου (John 8:12)

The equative verb, when elliptical, can be supplied from the context:

κεφαλὴ δὲ γυναικὸς ὁ ἀνήρ (1 Cor. 11:3)

5. When there is an imitation of a Hebraism, as the "construct state," in references using Yahweh's name genitivally, e.g., " . . . of the Lord":

λέγομεν ἐν λόγῳ κυρίου (1 Thess. 4:15)

καὶ νῦν ἰδοὺ χεὶρ κυρίου ἐπὶ σὲ (Acts 13:11)

ἐγένετο φωνὴ κυρίου (Acts 7:31)

ποτήριον κυρίου (1 Cor. 10:21)

TRANSLATION OF THE GREEK ARTICLE INTO ENGLISH

One cannot set up a simple rule of correspondences, translating by "the" only and always when the Greek article occurs, and never translating "a," or "an," since there is no indefinite article in Greek. It is much more complex than that. Here is why:

1. *Sometimes one must not translate the Greek article at all.*

δός μοι τοῦτο **τὸ** ὕδωρ (John 4:15)
τὸν Ἰακὼβ ἠγάπησα (Rom. 9:13)
ἀπὸ Ἰησοῦ Χριστοῦ, **ὁ** μάρτυς, **ὁ** πιστός (Rev. 1:5)
ὅτι **ὁ** θεὸς ἀγάπη ἐστίν (1 John 4:8)
καὶ **τὰ** νῦν, κύριε (Acts 4:29)

2. *Sometimes the (definite) article is translated better by the English indefinite article.* This is customary with the generic use of the article.

σὺ εἶ **ὁ** διδάσκαλος τοῦ Ἰσραὴλ (John 3:10)
οὐκ ἔχει ἐξουσίαν **ὁ** κεραμεὺς τοῦ πηλοῦ . . . ; (Rom. 9:21)
οὐδεὶς ἐπέβαλεν ἐπ᾽ αὐτὸν **τὴν** χεῖρα (John 7:30)

3. *Sometimes the article will be better translated by:*

a possessive pronoun—

᾽Ιησοῦς οὖν ἰδὼν **τὴν** μητέρα (John 19:26)

a relative pronoun—

ὁ ἄρτος **ὁ** ἐκ τοῦ οὐρανοῦ καταβαίνων (John 6:50)

a personal pronoun—

ὁ δὲ ἔφη αὐτοῖς· (Matt. 13:28)

4. *Sometimes the anarthrous construction in Greek will be served best by an articular translation into English.* (See the preceding section (pages 118–119) on Anarthrous Construction, numbers 3, 4, 5 for examples of expressions that normally will be more satisfactorily put into English by inclusion of the direct article.) Just one example will be given here—a Hebraism:

πνεῦμα κυρίου ἐπ᾽ ἐμὲ (Luke 4:18) *"The* Spirit of *the* Lord is upon me."

ARTICLES AND THE ATTRIBUTIVE POSITION

POSITIONS OF ATTRIBUTIVES: ADJECTIVES, ADJECTIVAL PARTICIPLES, & ADJECTIVAL PRONOUNS:

The *ascriptive* attributive positions:

article + adjective + noun
article + noun + adjective
adjective + article + noun
adjective + noun
noun + adjective
noun + article + adjective

καινοὺς δὲ οὐρανοὺς καὶ γῆν καινὴν κατὰ τὸ ἐπάγγελμα αὐτοῦ (2 Peter 3:13)
πᾶς γὰρ ὁ αἰτῶν (Luke 11:10)   ὁ κρατῶν τοὺς ἑπτὰ ἀστέρας (Rev. 2:1)
εἰρήνην τὴν ἐμὴν (John 14:27)   διαμεριζόμεναι γλῶσσαι (Acts 2:3)

The *restrictive* attributive position: article + noun + article + adjective

τοῦ λόγου τῆς ζωῆς (1 John 1:1)

The *predicative* attributive: used in the predicate with an equative verb, written or implied:

μακάριοι οἱ καθαροὶ τῇ καρδίᾳ (Matt. 5:8)

4

NEGATIVES, CONDITIONAL SENTENCES, PREPOSITIONS, ACCENTS, CONJUNCTIONS

NEGATIVES

1. *In general:* οὐ (οὐκ, οὐχι) is used with the Indicative mood as the objective negative adverb.

   μή (μήτι) is used with Subjn., Opt., Imv., Inf., and Ptc.

   οὐ δυνάμεθα γὰρ ἡμεῖς ἃ εἴδαμεν καὶ ἠκούσαμεν **μὴ** λαλεῖν (Acts 4:20)

2. *In questions:* οὐ (οὐχ, οὐχι) is used when an *affirmative* response was expected.

   οὐκ οἴδατε ὅτι . . . ; "Do not you know that . . . ?" [yes assumed] (Rom. 6:16)

   μή (μήτι) is used when a *negative* response was expected.

   μήτι ἐγώ εἰμι, κύριε; "It is not I, Lord, is it?" [no assumed]
   "Surely [it is] not I, Lord?"—*NIV* (Matt. 26:22)

   In the following example the main verb is already negative to which μή has been added so as to question doubtfully the whole negative idea:

   μὴ οὐκ ἤκουσαν; [μὴ was used here with the neg. ind. clause]
   "It is not that they have not heard, is it?" [no, assumed] (Rom. 10:18)

3. *In syntax:* the double negative = ordinary negative in English [not a double negative reversal].

   Καὶ ἐν ἐκείνῃ τῇ ἡμέρᾳ ἐμὲ **οὐκ** ἐρωτήσετε **οὐδέν** (John 16:23)
   [neg.   + neg. pron.]

   ἔθηκεν αὐτὸν ἐν μνήματι . . . οὗ **οὐκ** ἦν **οὐδεὶς οὔπω** κείμενος (Luke 23:53)

4. *In emphasis:* οὐ μή is used with the *aorist subjunctive* or *future indicative* to deny a future likelihood.

ὁ πιστεύων ἐπ᾽ αὐτῷ οὐ μὴ καταισχυνθῇ (1 Peter 2:6)

The negative conjunction οὐδέ can result in a triple negative in form, but with only a simple emphatic denial intended:

οὐ μή σε ἀνῶ **οὐδ᾽ οὐ μή** σε ἐγκαταλίπω (Heb. 13:5)

5. *In conditions:* οὐ is used in the protasis of Class 1. (example: p. 127—Luke 18:4b)
   μή is used in the protasis of Classes 2 and 3. (example: Class 2, p. 128—John 18:30)

6. *In exceptions:* μή is regularly used (εἰ + μή = "except").

μηδὲν . . , **εἰ μὴ** ῥάβδον μόνον (Mark 6:8)

7. *In single words:*

α (alpha privative) + noun or verb = un-, not (e.g., ἄκαρπος, ἀκαιρέομαι)
οὐδείς, οὐδεμία, οὐδέν = negative pronoun and adjective: none, no
οὐδέ (negative conjunction) and not, nor, also not, neither, not even
οὐδέποτε (adverb) never
οὐδέπω (adverb) not yet
οὐκέτι (adverb) no more, no longer, no further
οὔπω (adverb) not yet

NEGATIVES (Cont.)

οὔτε (adverb) and not; οὔτε . . . οὔτε neither . . . nor

οὐχί (intensive) of οὐ not, no, by no means

οὔ (particle) no: ὁ δὲ φησιν· οὔ (Matt. 13:29)

μηδαμῶς and μηθαμῶς (adverb) by no means, certainly not, no

μηδέ (neg. disjunctive particle) and not, nor, but not, not even

μηδείς, μηδεμία, μηδέν = neg. pronoun & adjective: nobody, nothing, no

μηδέποτε (adverb) never

μηδέπω (adverb) not yet

μηκέτι (adverb) no longer, not from now on

μήποτε (conjunction and particle) never, not . . . lest, whether perhaps

μήπου or μή που (conjunction) lest

μήπω (adverb) not yet

μήπως or μή πως (conjunction) not, lest somehow

μήτε (copula) and not; μήτε . . . μήτε neither . . . nor

μήτι (interrogative particle expecting a negative answer) not

CONDITIONAL SENTENCES

Conditional sentence: a complex sentence having a main clause and a subordinate "if" clause.

Protasis: the condition itself, i.e., the "if" clause.

Apodosis: the concluding result, i.e., the main clause of the sentence.

Order of Protasis and Apodosis: Either clause may come first or last.

Mood: basic determinant of the nature of the condition.

Types: There are four basic types:

Class 1: The "if" clause is assumed to be true.

Class 2: The "if" clause is assumed to be contrary to the fact.
If it contains a negative, the negative is treated as untrue.

Class 3: The "if" clause is assumed to be a possibility that could go either way.

Class 4: The "if" clause is assumed to be remotely possible.

CLASS ONE CONDITIONS

Construction of Class One Conditions:

Protasis	Apodosis
εἰ (normally) + Ind. mood (any tense)	Ind. (any tense)—normally.
ἐάν (occasionally)	But it may be:
negative: always οὐ, whenever used	Imv. (John 7:4; 8:39; 10:24; 20:15; Acts 4:9–10)
	Subjn. (John 7:23)—λυθῇ)

Kind of Condition:

Assumed to be true:

The argument builds on the indicative as *stating* a fact whether actual or hypothetical: "determined as fulfilled"—Robertson. "If" often means 'since' or 'even though' ('although') in Class One.

Illustrations:

εἰ δὲ ἐν πνεύματι θεοῦ ἐγὼ ἐκβάλλω τὰ δαιμόνια, ἄρα ἔφθασεν ἐφ᾽ ὑμᾶς ἡ βασιλεία τοῦ θεοῦ (Matt. 12:28) "If I expel demons by God's Spirit—and I do, therefore the . . ." or "Since I expel demons by God's Spirit, therefore the . . ."

εἴ τις ἔχει ὦτα ἀκούειν (protasis) ἀκουέτω (apodosis) (Mark 4:23)

εἰ καὶ τὸν θεὸν οὐ φοβοῦμαι οὐδὲ ἄνθρωπον ἐντρέπομαι . . . ἐκδικήσω αὐτήν . . . (Luke 18:4, 5) "Even though I do *not* fear God *nor* regard man . . . I will give her justice. . . . " [When the protasis has negatives as here (οὐ, οὐδὲ) it is assumed that the *negative* statements are true as negatively expressed. Here the judge was correct in saying he does *not* fear God.] Other examples with a negative—(John 10:37; Rev. 20:15).

Other Class One examples: future tense in both clauses (Matt. 26:33); past tenses in both clauses—aorist and imperfect (Acts 11:17); aorist tense in protasis, future in apodosis (Rom. 3:3).

CLASS TWO CONDITIONS

Construction of Class Two Conditions:

Protasis

εἰ + Ind. in a past tense

negative: μή whenever used in protasis; in apodosis οὐ may be used (Gal. 1:10)

Kind of Condition:

Assumed to be untrue; the argument states a premise whether actual or hypothetical, assumed to be *contrary to fact;* "determined as unfulfilled"—Robertson

Apodosis

ἄν (never first in clause) + Ind. in a past tense (ἄν sometimes omitted, e.g., John 15:22, if context makes a Class Two understanding necessary)

Time:

imperfect in protasis & apodosis = present time
aorist or pluperfect in protasis & apodosis = past time

Illustrations:

εἰ ἐκ τοῦ κόσμου ἦτε, ὁ κόσμος ἂν τὸ ἴδιον ἐφίλει (John 15:19) "If [right now] you were of the world, the world would love its own."

εἰ ἐν Τύρῳ καὶ Σιδῶνι ἐγένοντα αἱ δυνάμεις αἱ γενόμεναι ἐν ὑμῖν, πάλαι ἂν ἐν σάκκῳ καὶ σποδῷ μετενόησαν (Matt. 11:21). "If the miracles done among you had been done in Tyre and Sidon, they long ago would have repented in sackcloth and ashes."

εἰ μὴ ἦν οὗτος κακὸν ποιῶν, οὐκ ἄν σοι παρεδώκαμεν αὐτόν (John 18:30)

[It is assumed in the protasis that it is *not* that he was *not* doing evil; thus it is assumed that he was doing evil. This assumption was inaccurate in itself, but illustrates that grammatical constructions permit anything to be assumed. Note also the different negatives used in each clause. Finally note that no negatives are needed to have a contrary-to-fact, i.e., Class Two conditional sentence, as in the first two examples above.]

128

CLASS THREE CONDITIONS

Construction of Class Three Conditions:

Protasis	Apodosis
ἐάν (regularly) + Subjn. ἄν (shortened ἐάν, found in John occasionally) εἰ (rare) ἐάνπερ (Heb. 3:14; 6:3)	any form of the verb, but usually having futuristic predication: futuristic present Ind. future Ind. Imv.

negative: always μή, whenever used in the protasis

Kind of Condition:

Assumed to be an open question as to whether the condition will be met; the argument states an uncertainty; "undetermined with prospect of determination"—Robertson.

Translation: "If" suffices for translation in most cases.

Illustrations:

ἐάν τις διψᾷ ἐρχέσθω πρός με (John 7:37)

Περιτομὴ μὲν γὰρ ὠφελεῖ ἐὰν νόμον πράσσῃς (Rom. 2:25)

ἐὰν ὁμολογήσῃς . . . κύριον Ἰησοῦν καὶ πιστεύσῃς . . . ὅτι ὁ θεὸς αὐτὸν ἤγειρεν ἐκ νεκρῶν, σωθήσῃ (Rom. 10:9)

ἐάν τις ἀγαπᾷ τὸν κόσμον, οὐκ ἔστιν ἡ ἀγάπη τοῦ πατρὸς ἐν αὐτῷ (1 John 2:15)

CLASS FOUR CONDITIONS

Construction of Class Four Conditions:

Protasis   Apodosis

εἰ + Opt.   ἄν (never first in clause) + Opt.

Kind of Condition: *There is no complete example of Class Four in the LXX*
"remote prospect of determination"—Robertson   *or NT.*

Illustration:

ἀλλ' εἰ καὶ πάσχοιτε διὰ δικαιοσύνην, μακάριοι (1 Peter 3:14); see also Acts 20:16b.

INFORMAL IMPLIED CONDITIONS

1. The "condition" can be stated without using one of the four formal structures. An *imperative* with "and" is substituted.

πνεύματι περιπατεῖτε καὶ ἐπιθυμίαν σαρκὸς οὐ μὴ τελέσητε (Gal. 5:16)
[equivalent protasis]   [apodosis]

2. The "condition" may be implicit in the *adverbial* use of a *participle*.

πᾶν κτίσμα θεοῦ καλὸν καὶ οὐδὲν ἀπόβλητον μετὰ εὐχαριστίας λαμβανόμενον (1 Tim. 4:4)
[apodosis]   [protasis]

IRREGULARITIES IN THE USE OF CONDITIONS

Mixed Conditions:

The protasis of one class may be found sometimes with the apodosis of another class.

εἰ ἔχετε πίστιν ὡς κόκκον σινάπεως, ἐλέγετε ἂν τῇ συκαμίνῳ . . . (Luke 17:6)
(Class One protasis)   (Class Two apodosis)

Ἰουδαῖοι, οὓς ἔδει ἐπὶ σοῦ παρεῖναι καὶ κατηγορεῖν εἴ τι ἔχοιεν πρὸς ἐμέ (Acts 24:19)
(Class One or Two apodosis)   (Class Four protasis)

Elliptical Apodoses:

Only the protasis is stated because the apodosis is obviously implied.

[οὐδὲν κακὸν εὑρίσκομεν ἐν τῷ ἀνθρώπῳ τούτῳ] εἰ δὲ πνεῦμα ἐλάλησεν αὐτῷ ἢ ἄγγελος; [apodosis = what could we do about it anyway?] (Acts 23:9)

ἀμὴν λέγω ὑμῖν, εἰ δοθήσεται τῇ γενεᾷ ταύτῃ σημεῖον . . . [apodosis = it would contradict all that I am and stand for] (Mark 8:12). This elliptical apodosis in Mark 8:12 reproduces the Hebrew oath-type formula seen in 2 Sam. 11:11c; Gen. 42:15; Isa. 22:14. The meaning of the Hebrew idiom is emphatic negation. The closest parallel in English is the American frontier idiom: "I cross my heart and hope to die if . . . (so and so does not happen that the speaker has control over—usually a pledge of performance)."

PREPOSITIONS

A CONFIGURATION OF THE *SPACIAL* BASICS OF PREPOSITIONS

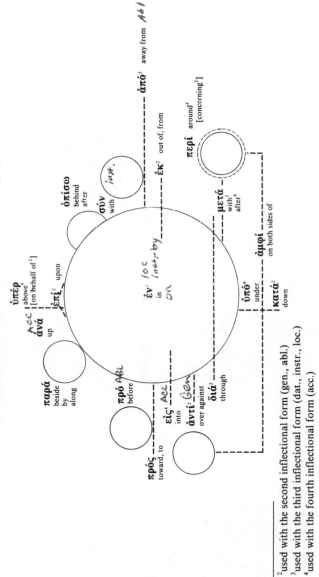

---

[2]used with the second inflectional form (gen., abl.)

[3]used with the third inflectional form (dat., instr., loc.)

[4]used with the fourth inflectional form (acc.)

ACCENTS

Accents:

´ = acute

` = grave

~ = circumflex

Backspacing Numbered Order of Syllables:

5 = fifth	syllable right to left	
4 = fourth	syllable right to left	
3 = third	syllable right to left (antepenult)
2 = second	syllable right to left (penult)
1 = first	syllable right to left (ultima)

General Rule for Nouns and Adjectives:

If the numbered syllable carries the accent, it will be:

5	4	3 (short)	2 (short)	1 (short)
n	n	´ (if 1 is short)	´	´ (punctuation or nothing follows)
o	o			` (another word, not an enclitic, follows)
n	n			
e	e			

5	4	3 (long)	2 (long)	1 (long)
n	n	` (if 1 is short)	~ (if 1 is short)	~ } pulled forward from 2 to 1
o	o		`	` }
n	n			` (another word, not an enclitic, follows)
e	e			

RECESSIVE ACCENTS IN VERBS

Syllables:	4	3	2	1	(backspace order)
	n o n e	´		short	λέ λυ κα
		(short or long)			ἐ πο ρεύ ον το
			´	long	λυ έ τω
			(short or long)		ἐ πο ρεύ θη
			~ long	short	λῦ ε / εὖ ρον
			´ all other instances		εἰ δό τες / λύ η
				~ long	ἦν, ἐλ θεῖν
			´ (only use of: εἰπὲ λόγῳ)	´ when followed by another word not enclitic	
				` (followed by punctuation or an enclitic)	. . . εἰσίν. ἠπίστησάν τινες,

Read "when" with each section of the chart. For example, (top line): When backspace syllable one—the ultima—is short, the acute accent falls on backspace syllable three, the antepenult; but (see λυέτω the third line of Greek) if backspace syllable one is long, the acute accent falls on syllable two.

Note: Rules of recessive accent do not apply to infinitives.

Note: Final -αι and -οι are considered short.

PROCLITICS AND ENCLITICS

Proclitics are those few short words that normally have no accent and 'lean forward' to be pronounced with the word that follows them:

ὁ, ἡ, οἱ, αἱ, εἰς, ἐν, ἐκ, ἐξ, ὡς, εἰ, οὐ, οὐκ, οὐχ.

They pick up an acute accent only in the rare instances when they receive one from a following enclitic, or when they occur as the last word in the sentence.

Enclitics consist of a small number of one- and two-syllable words that usually 'lean back' their accent to the word that precedes them. In a case where they cannot give their accent to the preceding word [two acutes cannot be placed on adjacent syllables], they may keep their accent, or lose it altogether. Many enclitics are found among the personal pronouns—μου [μή μου ἅπτου (John 20:17)], μοι, με, σου, σοι, σε—and the indefinite pronouns—τις, τι in all their forms (paradigm, p. 100). Other enclitics include most of the present-tense forms of the verb "to be": εἰμί, ἐστι(ν), ἐσμέν, ἐστέ, εἰσί(ν), and the verb φημί, φησί(ν). Besides these there are the enclitic particles ποτέ, πώς, γέ, τέ, and the enclitic adverb πού.

ILLUSTRATIONS OF ENCLITICS:

An acute is added to the ultima of the leaned-on word when:

Ἕλληνές τινες (John 12:20) the antepenult is accented.
γυναῖκές τινες (Luke 24:22) a circumflex is on the penult.
εἴς τινα κώμην (Luke 17:12) a proclitic precedes it.

ἱλασμός ἐστιν (1 John 2:2) a grave accent otherwise would be on the ultima.

An enclitic may keep its accent:

ἡμέρας τινάς (Acts 9:19) when a word cannot receive successive acutes.
τινὲς δὲ τῶν Φαρισαίων εἶπαν (Luke 6:2) when it begins a sentence.
εἰ μή τινές εἰσιν (Gal. 1:7) when it precedes another enclitic. τίνες became τινές.

An enclitic will normally lose its accent:

οὐδὲ τὸν πατέρα τις ἐπιγινώσκει (Matt. 11:27) when it is monosyllabic.
καί τινες (Mark 7:1) when it follows a word accented on the ultima.

CONJUNCTIONS

Coordinating Conjunctions connect words, phrases, and main clauses, including sentences, that are on a par with one another:

1. Simple coordinators:

καί ('and'), δέ ('and'), τε ('and'),
ἤ ('or'), εἴτε ('or')

2. Negative coordinators:

οὐδέ ('and not', 'not'), μηδέ ('and not'),
οὔτε ('and not', 'nor'),
μήτε ('and not', 'nor')

3. Adversative coordinators:

ἀλλά ('but'), δέ ('but')
πλήν ('but', 'nevertheless', 'however'),
μέντοι ('nevertheless'),
καίτοι ('and yet')

4. Inferential coordinators:

γάρ ('for'),
οὖν ('therefore'),
διό ('for this reason'), διότι ('therefore')
ἄρα (untranslated; used to introduce direct questions that build on what has gone
before = an emotional 'thus?')
ἄρα ('then', 'consequently', 'as a result')
δή ('indeed', 'therefore')
ὅθεν ('therefore', 'hence')

Subordinating Conjunctions connect dependent sentence elements, especially subordinate clauses to the main clause.

1. Purpose clauses: ἵνα ('for the purpose of', 'in order that')
ὅπως ('in order that')

2. Result clauses: ὥστε ('with the result that', 'so that')

3. Temporal clauses: ὅτε ('when', 'while', 'as long as')
ὅταν ('at the time that', 'whenever')
ἕως ('until')

4. Causal clauses: ὅτι ('because'), διότι ('because')
ἐπεί ('because', 'since'), ἐπειδέ ('since')

5. Conditional clauses: εἰ ('if', 'whether'), ἐάν ('if'),
εἴπερ ('if indeed')

6. Concessional clauses: κἄν ('even if', 'even though')

7. Comparative clauses: καθός ('just as'), καθάπερ ('just as')
ὡς ('as'), ὥσπερ ('[just] as')

8. Circumstantial clauses: ὅπου ('where'), οὗ ('where')

9. Statement clauses: ὅτι ('that' for indirect statement; or ". . ." when construed to be a direct statement—a *quotational* ὅτι)
ἔλεγον **ὅτι** γλεύκους μεμεστωμένοι εἰσίν (Acts 2:13)

138

5

THE TECHNIQUE OF TEXTUAL TRANSCRIPTION FOR GREEK EXEGESIS

Textual transcription is a syntactical technique that, having found the joints in a block of Greek text, emphasizes them by copying the text in biblical word order but in a new format. Grammatical relationships and syntactical structures are indicated by **subordination** and **parallelism**. The text always flows left to right down a line at a time at the appropriate junctures. The great benefit of this method is that it causes the main ideas to appear, hinged by the text's own transitions and parallels.

Textual transcription requires about 93% grammatical-syntactical skill and 7% art, in that decisions must be made in reference to allowable alternatives. This technique will not automatically solve the ambiguities in the grammar. However, it will make one acutely aware of them as he painstakingly decides the relationships intended by the biblical author within his texts.

Broad Working Principles for Textual Transcription

1. Copy the Greek text left to right only after having studied it thoroughly. Begin new sentences, unless bound tightly to subordinate or parallel networks, at the left margin.

2. Carefully consider every verb—the strongest element in each sentence. "Give each verb a break," i.e., its own line on which to stand with its modifiers, objects, and phrases. Exception: periphrastic verbs.

3. Decide which segments of the text begin a break and how they are to be lowered:

   (1) by *subordination*—placed down one line immediately *after* the last word of the preceding text.

   (2) by *parallelism*—placed down one line directly *under* any word, phrase, or clause with which it fits.

4. As little as one word may stand on a line (e.g., a vocative) or as much as a lengthy coherent simple sentence. The look of one's transposition will be determined *by the subject matter of the text*. In some cases, because of involved subordination, a second page will need to be joined horizontally to accommodate networks of subordinations in sequential systems. If one uses legal size paper ($8\frac{1}{2} \times 14$), writing horizontally on the 14" run, this will obviate the need, in most cases, to extend a second sheet out to the right side. In lieu of attaching such a sheet, one can back up the line that must follow to the right by placing it backspace flush with the right margin on the next line and drawing an arrow from the first word to that right margin where it should begin. Careful attention to parallels will restrict excessive horizontal flow and seldom make such measures necessary.

5. Avoid oversegmentation. Find the joints of the bony structure, but do not break any bones in the process. Retrace the author's own *syntactical* process without the obvious reductionism that he wrote only one word at a time.

6. Usually restudies of one's copied text will reveal a new insight, an inaccuracy, or an overlooked parallel. Make the changes. *Recopying* the page is Standard Operational Procedure (SOP) once, twice, or more.

7. Stylistic variations may be developed by the transposer by the use of side brackets, arrows, color codes, dotted oblique connections, and ideograms. These, strictly speaking, are not part of the transcription, but useful overlays.

2 Timothy 3:16–17 Transcribed

16 πᾶσα γραφὴ θεόπνευστος
    καὶ <u>ὠφέλιμος</u>   πρὸς διδασκαλίαν,
                    πρὸς ἐλεγμόν,
                    πρὸς ἐπανόρθωσιν,
                    πρὸς παιδείαν τὴν ἐν δικαιοσύνῃ,

17
                        ἵνα ἄρτιος ᾖ ὁ τοῦ θεοῦ ἄνθρωπος,
                    πρὸς πᾶν ἔργον ἀγαθὸν <u>ἐξηρτισμένος.</u>

1 Corinthians 11:2–5 Transcribed

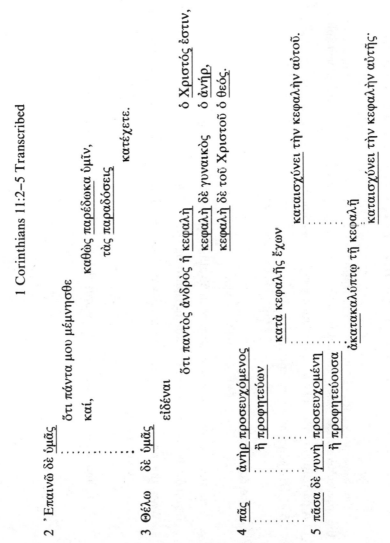

2 Ἐπαινῶ δὲ ὑμᾶς
....
    ὅτι πάντα μου μέμνησθε
    καί,
        καθὼς παρέδωκα ὑμῖν,
        τὰς παραδόσεις
            κατέχετε.

3 Θέλω   δὲ ὑμᾶς
  εἰδέναι
    ὅτι παντὸς ἀνδρὸς ἡ κεφαλὴ   ὁ Χριστός ἐστιν,
        κεφαλὴ δὲ γυναικὸς   ὁ ἀνήρ,
        κεφαλὴ δὲ τοῦ Χριστοῦ ὁ θεός.

4 πᾶς   ἀνὴρ προσευχόμενος
.... ἢ προφητεύων
      κατὰ κεφαλῆς ἔχων
           καταισχύνει τὴν κεφαλὴν αὐτοῦ.

5 πᾶσα δὲ γυνὴ προσευχομένη
      ἢ προφητεύουσα
        ἀκατακαλύπτῳ τῇ κεφαλῇ
           καταισχύνει τὴν κεφαλὴν αὐτῆς·

TECHNICAL GUIDELINES FOR TEXTUAL TRANSCRIPTION

The basic principles of textual transcription have already been set forth. What follows are some guidelines for the specific sequences whose format might not be readily apparent from the basic principles:

1. A participial *clause*, like a verb, should have its own line.

ὁ δὲ Ἡρῴδης ἰδὼν τὸν Ἰησοῦν
          ἐχάρη λίαν (Luke 23:8)

τοῦτο δὲ ἔλεγεν
      πειράζων αὐτόν (John 6:6)

2. A *substantival* participle may stay on line with its verb unless the verb is lowered for other reasons.

ὁ γὰρ ἀποθανὼν δεδικαίωται ἀπὸ τῆς ἁμαρτίας (Rom. 6:7)

3. When the independent clause repeats a word in a preceding subordinate clause, honor the parallelism first.

Εἰ ζῶμεν πνεύματι,
    πνεύματι καὶ στοιχῶμεν (Gal. 5:25)

[Note above how καὶ joins the two words that precede it, not the words before and after it.]

4. Likewise, if a conditional clause keys on a word in a preceding sentence, place it under the key word instead of in the normal left margin position for new sentences.

ὅτι ἐσμὲν τέκνα θεοῦ.
  εἰ δὲ τέκνα,
    καὶ κληρονόμοι [ἐσμέν] (Rom. 8:16–17)

5. When establishing a cognate parallel, let the internal parallel take precedence over that of lining up initial letters.

καὶ κληρονόμοι·
  κληρονόμοι μὲν θεοῦ,
  συγκληρονόμοι δὲ Χριστοῦ (Rom. 8:17)

[Note also that the last word above was moved one extra space to the right to establish yet another parallel.]

6. Prepositional phrases that are grammatically joined by a conjunction should be kept parallel even if their ideas are sequential.

ὁ θεὸς τὸν ἑαυτοῦ υἱὸν πέμψας ἐν ὁμοιώματι σαρκὸς ἁμαρτίας
                                    καὶ περὶ   ἁμαρτίας (Rom. 8:3)

7. An appositive (the second of juxtaposed nouns or noun equivalents related in the same way to the rest of the sentence and having no coordinating conjunction) should be kept on the same line.

. . . τὸ δὲ τέλος ζωὴν αἰώνιον (Rom. 6:22)

When there are plural appositives for a singular collective noun, they should be set in parallel, *but coordinately,* so as to reflect that apposition to the collective noun.

συνήχθη τὸ πρεσβυτέριον τοῦ λαοῦ,
ἀρχιερεῖς τε καὶ γραμματεῖς (Luke 22:66)

8. A clause or phrase set in the restrictive attributive position must *not* be paralleled below or subordinated.

ὁ ὄχλος πολὺς ὁ ἐλθὼν εἰς τὴν ἑορτήν . . . (John 12:12)

9. When a restrictive attributive series contains an appositive of the genitive case, then the appositive alone should be paralleled.

καὶ αὐτός ἐστιν ἡ κεφαλὴ τοῦ σώματος
τῆς ἐκκλησίας (Col. 1:18)

10. Whenever possible—always, if within a single sentence—keep a formal comparison parallel.

ἵνα ὥσπερ ἠγέρθη Χριστὸς ἐκ νεκρῶν . . .
οὕτως καὶ ἡμεῖς ἐν καινότητι ζωῆς περιπατήσωμεν (Rom. 6:4)

11. Put the relative pronoun *under the end of its antecedent* when it immediately follows it. If a preposition or parallels intervene, let it sit under the antecedent in the regular position at the beginning of the word.

ἀνδρί   (Luke 1:27)
ᾧ ὄνομα Ἰωσήφ

ἐν πᾶσιν τοῖς ἔθνεσιν   (Rom. 1:5, 6)

. . .   ἐν οἷς   ἐστε καὶ ὑμεῖς κλητοί

12. Subordination separates all subordinate clauses from independent clauses no matter which comes first.

εἴ τις ἐν λόγῳ οὐ πταίει,

        οὗτος τέλειος ἀνὴρ (James 3:2)

καλὸν ἦν αὐτῷ

    εἰ οὐκ ἐγεννήθη (Matt. 26:24)

13. A shift in mood from indicative to imperative requires subordination.

ἃ καὶ ἐμάθετε
: καὶ παρελάβετε
: καὶ ἠκούσατε
: καὶ εἴδετε ἐν ἐμοί,
<u>ταῦτα</u>   πράσσετε (Phil. 4:9)

14. Keep a periphrastic verb all together on one line.

ἵνα ἡ χαρὰ ἡμῶν πεπληρωμένη ᾖ (2 John 12)

15. If constraints of space are crucial, a subordinate clause may subordinate from its key word in the preceding clause rather than subordinating in the regular way at the end of it. In so doing, draw a hyphen-downline-hyphen to distinguish the subordination from parallelism.

λέγουσιν ⌐ αὐτῷ οἱ μαθηταί·
     └ ῥαββί, νῦν ἐζήτουν σε λιθάσαι οἱ Ἰουδαῖοι (John 11:8)

16. Show implied ellipsis by leaving space for it under the appropriate words of line one.

ἀλλ᾽ ἔχει καύχημα,
οὐ πρὸς θεόν (Rom. 4:2) .

τῷ γὰρ νόμῳ τοῦ θεοῦ οὐχ ὑποτάσσεται,
οὐδὲ   γὰρ δύναται (Rom. 8:7b)

Note well: Another time when more than one space between words will be found horizontally on a line occurs in the stretching of *either* a first or second line to accommodate two parallels:

μόλις γὰρ ὑπὲρ   δικαίου
        τις ἀποθανεῖται·
ὑπὲρ γὰρ τοῦ ἀγαθοῦ   (Rom. 5:7)

Whenever the horizontal space stretches out on a line a little finger's length or more—and the space does not indicate elliptical material from the line directly above—broken hyphens [- - - - -] may be used to direct the eye across the line to the parallel.

17. In a parallel phrase or clause in which only a part of the lowered line is parallel, underline the words in both lines that begin the parallel and let the preceding words of line two backspace from the underlined part.

διδάσκων αὐτοὺς ὡς ἐξουσίαν ἔχων
καὶ οὐχ ὡς οἱ γραμματεῖς (Mark 1:22)

18. Underlining:

(1) Underline parallels, if one or more lines intervene, and connect them by vertical dots.

ὅτι τοῖς <u>ἀγαπῶσιν</u> τὸν θεὸν

πάντα συνεργεῖ εἰς ἀγαθόν,

<u>τοῖς</u> κατὰ πρόθεσιν κλητοῖς οὖσιν. (Rom. 8:28)

(2) Underline parallels if those parallels are preceded or followed by other words on the line from which they should be distinguished.

προόρισεν συμμόρφους τῆς εἰκόνος τοῦ υἱοῦ αὐτοῦ,

εἰς τὸ <u>εἶναι αὐτὸν</u>

<u>πρωτότοκον</u> ἐν πολλοῖς ἀδελφοῖς (Rom. 8:29)

(3) Do not underline transparent parallels.

πέπεισμαι γὰρ

ὅτι οὔτε θάνατος

οὔτε ζωὴ

οὔτε ἄγγελοι

οὔτε ἀρχαί (Rom. 8:38)

(4) Underlining for emphasis on key concepts may be done in a different color and only after everything has been transcribed.

19. *Vertical dots* perpendicular to the lines of text may be used to connect parallels separated by more than one line. (The parallels so connected have already been underlined.) Such connections will often be synonymous parallels—in many cases, the same word. The columnar dots aid in tracing concepts through the passage. At the rewrite stage many of the possible ties will become apparent. The rule of thumb here is to honor sentence clarity and grammar first, and if long as well as short ties can be made smoothly, then do so. Dots connect the first letters of parallel words. A word with dots descending through the middle of it is not a part of the connection.

20. Keep intensive pronouns side by side with the word they intensify.

    Ἄρα οὖν αὐτὸς ἐγὼ τῷ μὲν νοΐ δουλεύω νόμῳ θεοῦ (Rom. 7:25)

21. Keep a hendiadys in spite of the καί all on the same line as would be expected.

    ἐν αὐτῇ εὐλογοῦμεν τὸν κύριον καὶ πατέρα (James 3:9)

22. There are three kinds of parallelism:

    synonymous (defining the key word, or repeating it)

    ἦν δὲ Μαριὰμ
    <u>ἡ ἀλείψασα</u> τὸν κύριον μύρῳ
    καὶ <u>ἐκμάξασα</u> τοὺς πόδας αὐτοῦ ταῖς θριξὶν αὐτῆς (John 11:2)

synthetical parallelism (adding elements, parts, qualities in sequence)

πολλοὶ . . . ἐληλύθεισαν πρὸς τὴν <u>Μάρθαν</u>

καὶ <u>Μαριάμ</u> (John 11:19)

antithetical (making any contrast: as of antonyms, negatives, or degrees)

εἰ ὁ θεὸς <u>ὑπὲρ</u> ἡμῶν,

. . . τίς

<u>καθ᾽</u> ἡμῶν; (Rom. 8:31)

ὥστε καὶ ὁ <u>γαμίζων</u> τὴν ἑαυτοῦ παρθένον <u>καλῶς</u>   ποιεῖ

καὶ ὁ <u>μὴ γαμίζων</u>   <u>κρεῖσσον ποιήσει</u> (1 Cor. 7:38)

23. Beware of superficial parallels.

καὶ μὴ καθὼς βλασφημούμεθα

καὶ   καθὼς φασίν τινες

. . .

καθὼς γέγραπται (Rom. 3:8–10; the third καθὼς is not parallel.)

150

Philippians 3:17–20 Transcribed

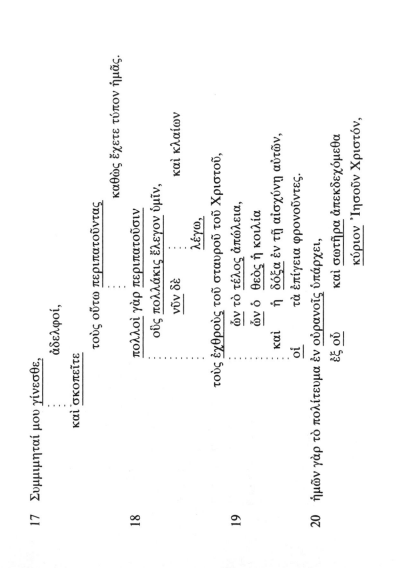

17 Συμμιμηταί μου γίνεσθε,
        ἀδελφοί,
   καὶ σκοπεῖτε
        τοὺς οὕτω περιπατοῦντας
            ..... καθὼς ἔχετε τύπον ἡμᾶς.

18 πολλοὶ γὰρ περιπατοῦσιν
        οὓς πολλάκις ἔλεγον ὑμῖν,   καὶ κλαίων
            νῦν δὲ ..... λέγω,
        ....
   τοὺς ἐχθροὺς τοῦ σταυροῦ τοῦ Χριστοῦ,

19   ὧν τὸ τέλος ἀπώλεια,
          ὧν ὁ θεὸς ἡ κοιλία
    καὶ   ἡ δόξα ἐν τῇ αἰσχύνῃ αὐτῶν,
    οἱ   τὰ ἐπίγεια φρονοῦντες.

20 ἡμῶν γὰρ τὸ πολίτευμα ἐν οὐρανοῖς ὑπάρχει,
   ἐξ οὗ   καὶ σωτῆρα ἀπεκδεχόμεθα
                κύριον Ἰησοῦν Χριστόν,

Luke 6:27–31 Transcribed

27 Ἀλλὰ ὑμῖν λέγω
τοῖς ἀκούουσιν·

  ἀγαπᾶτε τοὺς ἐχθροὺς ὑμῶν,
 καλῶς ποιεῖτε τοῖς μισοῦσιν ὑμᾶς,

28 εὐλογεῖτε τοὺς καταρωμένους ὑμᾶς,
προσεύχεσθε περὶ τῶν ἐπηρεαζόντων ὑμᾶς.

29   τῷ τύπτοντί σε ἐπὶ τὴν σιαγόνα
    .... καὶ τὴν ἄλλην,
 πάρεχε
   καὶ ἀπὸ τοῦ αἴροντός σου τὸ ἱμάτιον
            καὶ τὸν χιτῶνα μὴ κωλύσῃς.

30   παντὶ αἰτοῦντί σε
 δίδου,
   καὶ ἀπὸ τοῦ αἴροντός τὰ σὰ - - - - - - μὴ ἀπαίτει.

31 Καὶ καθὼς θέλετε
    ἵνα ποιῶσιν - - - - - - - ὑμῖν οἱ ἄνθρωποι
    ποιεῖτε - - - - - - - - - - - αὐτοῖς
 ὁμοίως.

A VERB BANK OF PRINCIPAL PARTS

6

PRESENT/A (-μαι=M)	FUTURE/A (-μαι=M)	AORIST/A (-μην=M)	PERFECT/A	PERFECT/M,P	AORIST/P
ἀγαλλιάω exult, be overjoyed	ἀγαλλιάσομαι	ἠγαλλίασα			ἠγαλλιάθην
ἀγαπάω love	ἀγαπήσω	ἠγάπησα	ἠγάπηκα	ἠγάπημαι	
ἀγγέλλω announce	ἀγγελῶ	ἤγγειλα	ἤγγελκα	ἤγγελμαι	ἠγγέλθην
ἁγιάζω sanctify		ἡγίασα		ἡγίασμαι	ἡγιάσθην
ἁγνίζω purify	ἁγνιῶ	ἥγνισα	ἥγνικα	ἥγνισμαι	ἡγνίσθην
ἀγνοέω be ignorant	ἀγνοήσω	ἠγνόησα	ἠγνόηκα	ἠγνόημαι	ἠγνοήθην
ἀγοράζω buy	ἀγοράσω	ἠγόρασα	ἠγόρακα	ἠγόρασμαι	ἠγοράσθην
ἄγω lead	ἄξω	ἤγαγον ἦξα	ἦχα ἀγήοχα	ἦγμαι	ἤχθην
ἀγωνίζομαι struggle	ἀγωνιοῦμαι	ἠγωνισάμηιν		ἠγώνισμαι	ἠγωνίσθην

ἀδικέω do wrong	ἀδικήσω	ἠδίκησα	ἠδίκηκα		ἠδικήθην
ἀθετέω nullify, reject	ἀθετήσω	ἠθέτησα			
αἱρέω choose	αἱρήσομαι	εἱλόμην εἱλάμην	ᾕρηκα	ᾕρημαι	ᾑρέθην
αἴρω take away	ἀρῶ	ἦρα	ἦρκα	ἦρμαι	ἤρθην
αἰσθάνομαι understand	αἰσθήσομαι	ᾐσθόμην		ᾔσθημαι	ᾐσθήθην
αἰτέω ask for	αἰτήσω	ᾔτησα	ᾔτηκα	ᾔτημαι	
ἀκολουθέω follow	ἀκολουθήσω	ἠκολούθησα	ἠκολούθηκα		
ἀκούω hear, listen	ἀκούσω	ἤκουσα	ἀκήκοα	ἤκουσμαι	ἠκούσθην
ἀλείφω anoint (for grooming)	ἀλείψω	ἤλειψα	ἀλήλιφα	ἀλήλιμμαι	ἠλείφθην
ἀλλάσσω change	ἀλλάξω	ἤλλαξα	ἤλλαχα	ἤλλαγμαι	ἠλλάχθην ἠλλάγην
ἁμαρτάνω sin	ἁμαρτήσω	ἥμαρτον ἡμάρτησα	ἡμάρτηκα	ἡμάρτημαι	ἡμαρτήθην

ἀναβαίνω go up	ἀναβήσομαι	ἀνέβην	ἀναβέβηκα		
ἀναβλέπω look up, see again	ἀναβλέψω	ἀνέβλεψα			
ἀναγγέλλω report, announce	ἀναγγελῶ	ἀνήγγειλα			ἀνηγγέλην
ἀναγινώσκω read	ἀναγνώσομαι	ἀνέγνων	ἀνέγνωκα	ἀνέγνωσμαι	ἀνεγνώσθην
ἀναγκάζω compel	ἀναγκάσω	ἠνάγκασα	ἠνάγκακα		ἠναγκάσθην
ἀνάγω lead or bring up	ἀνάξω	ἀνήγαγον			ἀνήχθην
ἀναιρέω take away	ἀναιρήσω ἀνελῶ	ἀνεῖλον ἀνεῖλα	ἀνῄρηκα	ἀνῄρημαι	ἀνῃρέθην
ἀνακλίνω recline	ἀνακλινῶ	ἀνέκλινα			
ἀνακρίνω examine	ἀνακρινῶ	ἀνέκρινα			ἀνεκρίθην
ἀναλαμβάνω take up	ἀναλήψομαι	ἀνέλαβον	ἀνείληφα		ἀνελήμφθην
ἀναλίσκω ἀναλόω consume	ἀναλώσω	ἀνήλωσα	ἀνήλωκα ἀνάλωκα	ἀνήλωμαι ἀνάλωμαι	ἀνηλώθην

Present	Future	Aorist	Perfect Active	Perfect Mid./Pass.	Aorist Passive
ἀναπαύω rest	ἀναπαύσω	ἀνέπαυσα		ἀναπέπαυμαι	ἀνεπαύθην
ἀναστρέφω behave	ἀναστρέψω	ἀνέστρεψα		ἀνέστραμμαι	ἀνεστράφην
ἀνατέλλω rise	ἀνατελῶ	ἀνέτειλα	ἀνατέταλκα		
ἀνατρέφω train		ἀνέθρεψα		ἀνατέθραμμαι	ἀνετράφην
ἀναφέρω bring up	ἀνοίσω	ἀνήνεγκα / ἀνήνεγκον			
ἀνέχω endure	ἀνέξομαι	ἀνέσχον / ἠνεσχόμην	ἀνέσχηκα		
ἀνθίστημι withstand		ἀντέστην	ἀνθέστηκα		ἀντεστάθην
ἀνίημι abandon	ἀνήσω	ἀνῆκα	ἀνεῖκα	ἀνεῖμαι	ἀνέθην
ἀνίστημι rise, raise	ἀναστήσω	ἀνέστησα / ἀνέστην	ἀνέστακα		
ἀνοίγω open	ἀνοίξω	ἀνέῳξα / ἠνέῳξα / ἤνοιξα	ἀνέῳγα	ἀνέῳγμαι / ἠνέῳγμαι	ἀνεῴχθην / ἠνοίχθην / ἠνεῴχθην / ἠνοίγην
ἀντιλέγω contradict, oppose	ἀντιλέξω	ἀντεῖπον	ἀντείρηκα		

Present	Future	Aorist	Perfect active	Perfect mid/pass	Aorist passive
ἀξιόω to be [or make] worthy	ἀξιόσω	ἠξίωσα		ἠξίωμαι	ἠξιώθην
ἀπαγγέλλω proclaim, announce	ἀπαγγελῶ	ἀπήγγειλα			ἀπηγγέλην
ἀπαλλάσσω release	ἀπαλλάξω	ἀπήλλαξα	ἀπήλλαχα	ἀπήλλαγμαι	ἀπηλλάγην
ἀπαντάω meet	ἀπαντήσω	ἀπήντησα	ἀπήντηκα	ἀπήντημαι	
ἀπαρνέομαι deny	ἀπαρνήσομαι	ἀπηρνησάμην		ἀπήρνημαι	
ἀπέχω receive, be distant, refrain	ἀφέξομαι	ἀπέσχον			
ἀποβάλλω throw away	ἀποβαλῶ	ἀπέβαλον	ἀποβέβληκα		ἀπεβλήθην
ἀποδίδωμι give away	ἀποδόσω	ἀπέδωκα / ἀπεδόμην			ἀπεδόθην
ἀποθνῄσκω die	ἀποθανοῦμαι	ἀπέθανον			
ἀποκαθίστημι / ἀποκαθιστάνω restore	ἀποκαταστήσω	ἀπεκατέστην			ἀπεκατεστάθην (note: double aug.)
ἀποκαλύπτω uncover, reveal	ἀποκαλύψω	ἀπεκάλυψα			ἀπεκαλύφθην

Present	Future	Aorist	Perfect Active	Perfect M/P	Aorist Passive
ἀποκρίνομαι answer	ἀποκρινῶ	ἀπεκρινάμην			ἀπεκρίθην
ἀποκτείνω ἀποκτέννω kill	ἀποκτενῶ	ἀπέκτεινα ἀπέκτανον ἀπεκτάμην	ἀπέκτονα ἀπεκτόνηκα ἀπέκτακα		ἀπεκτάνθην
ἀπολαμβάνω receive	ἀπολήμψομαι	ἀπέλαβον			
ἀπόλλυμι ἀπόλλυμαι destroy	ἀπολέσω ἀπολῶ ἀπολοῦμαι	ἀπόλεσα ἀπωλόμην	ἀπόλωλεκα ἀπόλωλα		
ἀπολογέομαι speak in defense		ἀπελογησάμην		ἀπολελόγημαι	ἀπελογήθην
ἀπορέω be in doubt, uncertain		ἠπόρησα	ἠπόρηκα	ἠπόρημαι	ἠπορήθην
ἀποστέλλω send out	ἀποστελῶ	ἀπέστειλα	ἀπέσταλκα	ἀπέσταλμαι	ἀπεστάλην
ἀποστερέω rob		ἀπεστέρησα		ἀπεστέρημαι	
ἀποστρέφω turn away	ἀποστρέψω	ἀπέστρεψα		ἀπέστραμμαι	ἀπεστράφην
ἀποτίθημι put off		ἀπεθέμην			ἀπετέθην
ἀποφέρω carry away		ἀπήνεγκα			ἀπηνέχθην

Present	Future	Aorist	Perfect Active	Perfect Mid/Pass	Aorist Passive
ἅπτω (kindle, touch)	ἅψω	ἦψα		ἦμμαι	ἡρέσθην
ἀρέσκω (please)	ἀρέσω	ἤρεσα	ἀρήρεκα		
ἀρκέω (be sufficient, content)	ἀρκέσω	ἤρκεσα		ἤρκεσμαι	ἠρκέσθην
ἁρμόζω (join)	ἁρμόσω	ἥρμοσα	ἥρμοκα	ἥρμοσμαι	ἡρμόσθην / ἁρμόχθην
ἀρνέομαι (deny)	ἀρνήσομαι	ἠρνησάμην		ἤρνημαι	
ἁρπάζω (snatch)	ἁρπάσω	ἥρπασα	ἥρπακα	ἥρπασμαι	ἡρπάσθην / ἡρπάγην
ἄρχω (be first, rule)	ἄρξομαι	ἠρξάμην	ἦρχα	ἦργμαι	ἤρχθην
ἀσθενέω (be weak)	[ἀσθενήσω]	ἠσθένησα			
ἀτιμάζω (dishonor, insult)	ἀτιμάσω	ἠτίμασα	ἠτίμακα	ἠτίμασμαι	ἠτιμάσθην
αὐλίζομαι (lodge, stay)		ηὐλισάμην		ηὔλισμαι	ηὐλίσθην
αὐξάνω / αὔξω (grow)	αὐξήσω / αὐξανῶ	ηὔξησα	ηὔξηκα	ηὔξημαι	ηὐξήθην

ἀφαιρέω take away	ἀφελῶ	ἀφεῖλον	ἀφῄρηκα	ἀφῄρημαι	ἀφῃρέθην
ἀφίημι let go, forgive	ἀφήσω	ἀφῆκα	ἀφεῖκα	ἀφεῖμαι	ἀφέθην ἀφείθην
ἀφίστημι mislead, fall away	ἀποστήσω	ἀπέστησα ἀπέστην			
ἀφορίζω set apart	ἀφορίσω ἀφοριῶ	ἀφώρισα		ἀφώρισμαι	ἀφορίσθην
βάλλω throw	βαλῶ	ἔβαλον	βέβληκα	βέβλημαι	ἐβλήθην
βαπτίζω immerse, baptize	βαπτίσω	ἐβάπτισα		βεβάπτισμαι	ἐβαπτίσθην
βάπτω dip	βάψω	ἔβαψα		βέβαμμαι	ἐβάφην
βαρέω weigh down	βαρήσω	ἐβάρησα	βεβάρηκα	βεβάρημαι	ἐβαρήθην
βασανίζω torture, examine	βασανιῶ	ἐβασάνισα		βεβασάνισμαι	ἐβασανίσθην
βασιλεύω rule	βασιλεύσω	ἐβασίλευσα			
βαστάζω bear	βαστάσω βαστάξω	ἐβάστασα ἐβάσταξα		βεβάσταγμαι	ἐβαστάχθην
βδελύσσομαι abhor, detest	βδελύξομαι	ἐβδελυξάμην		ἐβδέλυγμαι	ἐβδελύχθην

βεβαιόω make firm	βεβαιόω	ἐβεβαίωσα			ἐβεβαιώθην
βιάζω apply force		ἐβιασάμην		βεβίασμαι	ἐβιάσθην
βλαστάνω βλαστάω bud, sprout	βλαστήσω	ἔβλασον ἐβλάστησα	βεβλάστηκα		
βλασφημέω revile		ἐβλασφήμησα	βεβλασφήμηκα		ἐβλασφημήθην
βλέπω see	βλέψω	ἔβλεψα	βέβλεφα βέβλοφα	βέβλεμμαι	ἐβλέφθην
βοάω shout	βοήσω	ἐβόησα	βεβόηκα	βεβόημαι	ἐβόσθην
βοηθέω help	βοηθήσομαι	ἐβοήθησα			ἐβοήθην
βόσκω graze, feed, tend	βοσκήσω	ἐβόσκησα	βεβόσκηκα		ἐβοσκήθην
βουλεύω resolve	βουλεύσομαι	ἐβουλευσάμην	βεβούλευκα	βεβούλευμαι	
βούλομαι want	βουλήσομαι			βεβούλημαι	ἐβουλήθην
βρέχω send rain	βρέξω	ἔβρεξα		βέβρεγμαι	ἐβρέχθην ἐβράχην

γαμέω marry	γαμῶ	ἔγημα ἐγάμησα ἐγέμισα	γεγάμηκα	γεγάμημαι	ἐγαμήθην
γεμίζω fill	γεμίσω				ἐγεμίσθην
γεννάω beget, bear	γεννήσω	ἐγέννησα	γεγέννηκα	γεγέννημαι	ἐγεννήθην
γεύομαι taste	γεύσομαι	ἐγευσάμην		γέγευμαι	
γίνομαι become	γενήσομαι	ἐγενόμην	γέγονα	γεγένημαι	ἐγενήθην
γινώσκω experience	γνώσομαι	ἔγνων	ἔγνωκα	ἔγνωσμαι	ἐγνώσθην
γνωρίζω make known	γνωρίσω	ἐγνώρισα	ἐγνώρικα		ἐγνωρίσθην
γογγύζω murmur, whisper in secret	γογγύσω	ἐγόγγυσα			
γράφω write	γράψω	ἔγραψα	γέγραφα γεγράφηκα ἐγρήγορα	γέγραμμαι	ἔγραφην ἐγράφθην ἐγρηγορήθην
γρηγορέω keep awake, alert	γρηγορήσω	ἐγρηγόρησα			
δαπανάω spend, use up	δαπανήσω	ἐδαπάνησα		δεδαπάνημαι	

Present / meaning	Future	Aorist	Perfect Active	Perfect Mid/Pass	Aorist Passive
δείκνυμι δεικνύω show	δείξω	ἔδειξα	δέδειχα	δέδειγμαι	ἐδείχθην
δειπνέω eat a dinner	δειπνήσω	ἐδείπνησα	δεδείπνηκα		
δέομαι ask, beg	δεήσομαι				ἐδεήθην
δέρω beat, skin	δερῶ	ἔδειρα		δέδαρμαι	ἐδάρην
δέχομαι welcome	δέξομαι	ἐδεξάμην		δέδεγμαι	ἐδέχθην
δέω bind	δήσω	ἔδησα	δέδεκα	δέδεμαι	ἐδέθην
δηλόω make clear	δηλώσω	ἐδήλωσα		δεδήλωμαι	ἐδηλώθην
διακονέω serve	διακονήσω	διηκόνησα			διηκονήθην
διακρίνω distinguish, dispute	διακρινῶ				διεκρίθην
διαλέγομαι discuss	διαλέξομαι	διελεξάμην		διείλεγμαι	διελέχθην διελέγην
διαμαρτύρομαι warn, witness		διεμαρτυράμην		διαμεμαρτύρημαι	
διαμερίζω divide, distribute		διεμέρισα			διεμερίσθην

Present	Future	Aorist	Perfect Active	Perfect Mid./Pass.	Aorist Passive
διανοίγω open, explain		διήνοιξα			διηνοίχθην
διατάσσω command	διατάξομαι	διέταξα	διατέταχα		διετάχθην
διαφέρω carry through, differ	διοίσω	διήνεγκα διήνεγκον			
διδάσκω teach	διδάξω	ἐδίδαξα	δεδίδαχα	δεδίδαγμαι	ἐδιδάχθην
δίδωμι give	δώσω	ἔδωκα	δέδωκα	δέδομαι	ἐδόθην
διέρχομαι go through	διελεύσομαι	διῆλθον	διελήλυθα		
δικαιόω justify	δικαιώσω	ἐδικαίωσα		δεδικαίωμαι	ἐδικαιώθην
διψάω thirst	διψήσω	ἐδίψησα	δεδίψηκα		
διώκω pursue	διώξω	ἐδίωξα	δεδίωχα	δεδίωμαι	ἐδιώχθην
δοκέω seem	δόξω	ἔδοξα	δέδοχα	δέδογμαι	ἐδόχθην
δοκιμάζω test, approve	δοκιμάσω	ἐδοκίμασα		δεδοκίμασμαι	
δοξάζω glorify	δοξάσω	ἐδόξασα		δεδόξασμαι	ἐδοξάσθην

Present	Future 1-6	Aorist	Perfect	Perf. M/P	Aorist Pass.
δουλεύω be a slave	δουλεύσω	ἐδούλευσα	δεδούλευκα		
δουλόω enslave	δουλώσω	ἐδούλωσα		δεδούλωμαι	ἐδουλώθην
δύναμαι be able, can	δυνήσομαι	ἐδυνησάμην		δεδύνημαι	ἐδυνήθην / ἠδυνάσθην
ἐάω (ἐῶ) let	ἐάσω	εἴασα	εἴακα	εἴαμαι	εἴαθην
ἐγγίζω approach	ἐγγιῶ	ἤγγισα	ἤγγικα		
ἐγείρω rouse, raise up	ἐγερῶ	ἤγειρα	ἐγήγερκα	ἐγήγερμαι	ἠγέρθην
ἐγκαταλείπω abandon	ἐγκαταλείψω	ἐγκατέλιπον			ἐγκατελείφθην

εἶδον: used only as 2 aor. of ὁράω: ἴδον see

cf. εἴδαμεν εἶδαν   subjn. ἴδω   imv. ἴδε
                inf. ἰδεῖν   ptc. ἰδών

Present 1-6:
εἰμί—I am
εἶ
ἐστί(ν)
ἐσμέν
ἐστέ
εἰσί(ν)

Future 1-6:
ἔσομαι—I shall be
ἔσῃ
ἔσται
ἐσόμεθα
ἔσεσθε
ἔσονται

Imperfect 1-6:
ἤμην—I was
ἦς, ἦσθα
ἦν
ἦμεν, ἤμεθα
ἦτε
ἦσαν

Present Infinitive:
εἶναι—to be

Future infinitive:
ἔσεσθαι—going to be

Participle Bases:
ὤν, οὖσα, ὄν
(m) (f) (n)

Imperatives
ἴσθι—be (2 s.)
ἔστε (2 pl.)
ἔστω, ἤτω (3 s.)
ἔστωσαν (3 pl.)

Future Ptc.
ἐσόμενος, -η, -ον

Subjunc. 1-6:
ὦ—I might be
ᾖς
ᾖ
ὦμεν
ἦτε
ὦσι

Opt. (3 s.) εἴη

[εἶπον] (λέγω, φημί)	ἐρῶ	εἶπον / εἶπα (takes first or second aorist endings)	εἴρηκα	εἴρημαι	ἐρρέθην
say					
ἐκβάλλω	ἐκβαλῶ	ἐξέβαλον	ἐκβέβληκα		ἐξεβλήθην
expel					
ἐκδικέω	ἐκδικήσω	ἐξεδίκησα			
avenge					
ἐκκόπτω	ἐκκόψω	ἐξέκοψα			ἐξεκόπην
cut off					
ἐκλέγομαι		ἐξελεξάμην		ἐκλέλεγμαι	
choose					
ἐκπίπτω	ἐκπεσοῦμαι	ἐξέπεσα / ἐξέπεσον	ἐκπέπτωκα		
fall from					
ἐκπλήσσω		ἐξέπληξα			ἐξεπλάγην
astound					
ἐκτείνω	ἐκτενῶ	ἐξέτεινα			
stretch out					
ἐκχέω	ἐκχεῶ	ἐξέχεα	ἐκκέχυκα	ἐκκέχυμαι	ἐξεχύθην
ἐκχύν(ν)ω		ἐκχυσθην			
pour out					
ἐλέγχω	ἐλέγξω	ἤλεγξα		ἐλήλεγμαι	ἠλέγχθην
convince					
ἐλεέω	ἐλεήσω	ἠλέησα		ἠλέημαι	ἠλεήθην
have mercy					

Present (meaning)	Future	Aorist	Perfect Active	Perfect Mid/Pass	Aorist Passive
ἐλευθερόω — set free	ἐλευθερώσω	ἠλευθέρωσα			ἠλευθερώθην
ἕλκω, ἑλκύω — drag, draw	ἑλκύσω, ἕλξω	εἵλκυσα, εἷλξα	εἵλκυκα	εἵλκυσμαι	εἱλκύσθην, εἵλχθην
ἐλπίζω — hope	ἐλπιῶ, ἐλπίσω	ἤλπισα	ἤλπικα	ἤλπισμαι	ἠλπίσθην
ἐμβριμάομαι, ἐμβριμόομαι — snort, censure, be filled with emotion		ἐνεβριμησάμην			ἐνεβριμήθην
ἐμπαίζω — make fun of	ἐμπαίξω	ἐνέπαιξα	ἐμπέπαιχα		ἐνεπαίχθην
ἐμπί(μ)πλημι, ἐμπι(μ)πλάω — fill		ἐνέπλησα		ἐμπέπλησμαι	ἐνεπλήσθην
ἐμφανίζω — make visible	ἐμφανίσω	ἐνεφάνισα	ἐμπεφάνικα		ἐνεφανίσθην
ἐνδύω — clothe	ἐνδύσομαι	ἐνέδυσα	ἐνδέδυκα	ἐνδέδυμαι	
ἐνεργέω — work		ἐνήργησα	ἐνήργηκα		
ἐντέλλομαι — command	ἐντελοῦμαι	ἐνετειλάμην		ἐντέταλμαι	

Present	Future	Aorist	Perfect Active	Perfect Mid/Pass	Aorist Passive
ἐξίστημι ἐξιστάνω confuse, amaze		ἐξέστησα ἐξέστην	ἐξέστακα	ἐξίσταμαι	
ἐξουθενέω – όω ἐξουδενέω – όω despise, disdain		ἐξουθένησα		ἐξουθένημαι	ἐξουθενήθην ἐξουδενήθην
ἐπαγγέλλομαι promise, profess		ἐπηγγειλάμην		ἐπήγγελμαι	ἐπηγγέλθην
ἐπαίρω lift up	ἐπαρῶ	ἐπῆρα	ἐπῆρκα		ἐπήρθην
ἐπερωτάω ask	ἐπερωτήσω	ἐπηρώτησα			ἐπερωτήθην
ἐπιγινώσκω know exactly	ἐπιγνώσομαι	ἐπέγνων	ἐπέγνωκα		ἐπεγνώσθην
ἐπιθυμέω desire	ἐπιθυμήσω	ἐπεθύμησα			
ἐπικαλέω name, call upon	ἐπικαλέσομαι	ἐπεκάλεσα		ἐπικέκλημαι	ἐπεκλήθην
ἐπισκέπτομαι visit, examine	ἐπισκέψομαι	ἐπεσκεψάμην ἐπεσκόπασα		ἐπέσκεμμαι	
ἐπίσταμαι be acquainted with	ἐπιστήσομαι				ἠπιστήθην
ἐπιστρέφω turn around, return	ἐπιστρέψω	ἐπέστρεψα	ἐπέστροφα		ἐπεστράφην

Present	Future	Aorist	Perfect Active	Perfect Mid./Pass.	Aorist Passive
ἐπιτελέω accomplish	ἐπιτελέσω	ἐπετέλεσα			
ἐπιτίθημι put upon	ἐπιθήσω	ἐπέθηκα κ aor. ἐπέθην 2 aor. ἐπεθέμην mid.		ἐπιτέθειμαι	ἐπετέθην
ἐργάζομαι work, do	ἐργάσομαι	ἠργασάμην εἰργασάμην		εἴργασμαι	εἰργάσθην
ἔρχομαι come, go	ἐλεύσομαι	ἦλθον ἦλθα	ἐλήλυθα		
ἐρωτάω question, ask	ἐρωτήσω	ἠρώτησα	ἠρώτηκα		
ἐσθίω ἔσθω eat	φάγομαι ἔδομαι	ἔφαγον			
ἑτοιμάζω prepare	ἑτοιμάσω	ἡτοίμασα	ἡτοίμακα	ἡτοίμασμαι	ἡτοιμάσθην
εὐαγγελίζω bring good news	εὐαγγελίσω	εὐηγγέλισα		εὐηγγέλισμαι	εὐηγγελίσθην
εὐλογέω praise, bless	εὐλογήσω	εὐλόγησα	εὐλόγηκα	εὐλόγημαι	εὐλογήθην
εὑρίσκω find	εὑρήσω	εὗρον εὑράμην εὕρησα	εὕρηκα	ηὕρημαι εὕρημαι	εὑρέθην ηὑρέθην

Present	Future	Aorist	Perfect Active	Perfect Mid/Pass	Aorist Passive
εὐφραίνω cheer, enjoy oneself	εὐφρανῶ	εὔφρανα / ηὔφρανα			εὐφράνθην / ηὐφράνθην
εὐχαριστέω give thanks		εὐχαρίστησα			εὐχαριστήθην
ἐφίστημι stand near		ἐπέστην	ἐφέστακα	ἐπίσταμαι	ἐπεστάθην
ἔχω have, hold	ἕξω	ἔσχον / ἔσχησα	ἔσχηκα	ἔσχημαι	ἐσχέθην
ζάω (ζῶ) live	ζήσω	ἔζησα			
ζημιόω inflict punishment, injury	ζημιώσω	ἐζημίωσα	ἐζημίωκα	ἐζημίωμαι	ἐζημιώθην
ζητέω seek	ζητήσω	ἐζήτησα	ἐζήτηκα		
ζῳοποιέω make alive	ζῳοποιήσω				ἐζῳοποιήθην
ἡγέομαι guide	ἡγήσομαι	ἡγησάμην		ἥγημαι	ἡγήθην
ἥκω be present	ἥξω	ἦξα	ἦκα		
ἡσυχάζω keep quiet, be at rest	ἡσυχάσω	ἡσύχασα			
θανατόω put to death	θανατόσω	ἐθανάτωσα	τεθανάτοκα	τεθανάτομαι	ἐθανατώθην

170

θάπτω bury	θάψω	ἔθαψα		τέθαμμαι	ἐθάφθην ἐτάφην
θαυμάζω wonder	θαυμάσομαι	ἐθαύμασα	τεθαύμακα	τεθαύμασμαι	ἐθαυμάσθην
θεάομαι look at	θεάσομαι	ἐθεασάμην		τεθέαμαι	ἐθεάθην
θέλω = ἐθέλω wish, will	θελήσω ἐθελήσω	ἠθέλησα ἔθελησα	ἠθέληκα τεθέληκα		ἐθελήθην
θεμελιόω lay a foundation	θεμελιώσω	ἐθεμελίωσα		τεθεμελίωμαι	
θεραπεύω serve, treat, heal	θεραπεύσω	ἐθεράπευσα		τεθεράπευμαι	ἐθεραπεύθην
θερίζω harvest	θερίσω	ἐθέρισα		τεθέρισμαι	ἐθερίσθην
θησαυρίζω store up		ἐθησαύρισα		τεθησαύρισμαι	
θλίβω press upon, oppress	θλίψω	ἔθλιψα	τέθλιφα	τέθλιμμαι	ἐθλίβην ἐθλίφθην
θνῄσκω die, be dead	θανοῦμαι θνήξομαι	ἔθανον	τέθνηκα		
θριαμβεύω triumph		ἐθριάμβευσα	τεθριάμβευκα		
θύω sacrifice	θύσω	ἔθυσα	τέθυκα	τέθυμαι	ἐτύθην

	Future	Aorist	Perfect Active	Perfect Mid/Pass	Aorist Passive
ἰάομαι heal, cure	ἰάσομαι	ἰασάμην		ἴαμαι	ἰάθην
ἵστημι ἱστάνω stand	στήσω	ἔστησα ἔστην	ἔστηκα	ἔσταμαι	ἐστάθην
ἰσχύω be strong	ἰσχύσω	ἴσχυσα	ἴσχυκα		ἰσχύθην
καθαιρέω take down	καθελῶ	καθεῖλον καθεῖλα			
καθαρίζω cleanse	καθαριῶ	ἐκαθάρισα		κεκαθάρισμαι	ἐκαθαρίσθην ἐκαθερίσθην
καθεύδω sleep	καθευδήσω	ἐκαθεύδησα			
καθίζω sit, seat	καθίσω καθέσω καθιῶ	ἐκάθισα	κακάθικα		
καθίστημι καθιστάνω appoint	καταστήσω	κατέστησα	καθέστακα καθέστηκα	καθέσταμαι	κατεστάθην
καίω burn	καύσω	ἔκαυσα	κέκαυκα	κέκαυμαι κέκαυσμαι	ἐκαύθην ἐκάην
καλέω call	καλέσω	ἐκάλεσα	κέκληκα	κέκλημαι	ἐκλήθην

Present	Future	Aorist	Perfect Active	Perfect Mid/Pass	Aorist Passive
καλύπτω conceal	καλύψω	ἐκάλυψα		κεκάλυμμαι	ἐκαλύφθην
κάμπτω bend, bow	κάμψω	ἔκαμψα			ἐκάμφθην
καταβαίνω go down	καταβήσομαι	κατέβην	καταβέβηκα		
καταγγέλλω proclaim		κατήγγειλα	κατήγγελκα		κατηγγέλην
καταισχύνω disgrace	καταισχυνῶ			κατῄσχυμμαι	κατῃσχύνθην
κατακαίω burn down	κατακαύσω	κατέκαυσα	κατακέκαυκα		κατεκάην κατεκαύθην
κατακρίνω condemn	κατακρινῶ	κατέκρινα			κατεκρίθην
καταλαμβάνω attain	καταλήψομαι	κατέλαβον	κατείληφα	κατείλημμαι κατείληπται	κατελήμφθην
καταλείπω leave behind	καταλείψω	κατέλειψα κατέλιπον	καταλέλοιπα	καταλέλειμμαι	κατελείφθην
καταλλάσσω reconcile		κατήλλαξα			κατηλλάγην
καταντάω arrive		κατήντησα	κατήντηκα		
καταπατέω trample	καταπατήσω	κατεπάτησα			κατεπατήθην

καταπίνω swallow	καταπιοῦμαι	κατέπιον	καταπέπωκα		κατεπόθην
καταργέω abolish	καταργήσω	κατήργησα	κατήργηκα	κατήργημαι	κατηργήθην
καταρτίζω make complete, create	καταρτίσω	κατήρτισα		κατήρτισμαι	
κατασκευάζω prepare, construct	κατασκευάσω	κατεσκεύασα		κατεσκεύασμαι	κατεσκευάσθην
καταφρονέω treat with contempt	καταφρονήσω	κατεφρόνησα			κατεφρονήθην
κατεργάζομαι achieve	κατεργάσομαι	κατειργασάμην			κατειργάσθην
κατεσθίω consume	καταφάγομαι	κατέφαγον	κατεδήδοκα	κατεδήδεσμαι	κατηδέσθην
κατέδομαι					
κατέχω hold down	καθέξω	κατέσχον			
	κατασχήσω	κατέσχα			
κατηγορέω accuse	κατηγορήσω	κατηγόρησα			
κατηχέω make oneself understood, inform	κατηχήσω	κατήχησα		κατήχημαι	κατηχήθην
κατοικέω inhabit, dwell	κατοικήσω	κατῴκησα			

Present	Future	Aorist	Perfect Active	Perfect M/P	Aorist Passive
καυματίζω burn		ἐκαυμάτισα			ἐκαυματίσθην
καυχάομαι boast	καυχήσομαι	ἐκαυχησάμην		κεκαύχημαι	
κελεύω command, urge	κελεύσω	ἐκέλευσα	κεκέλευκα	κεκέλευσμαι	ἐκελεύσθην
κενόω make empty	κενώσω	ἐκένωσα	κεκένωκα	κεκένωμαι	ἐκενώθην
κερδαίνω gain	κερδήσω κερδανῶ	ἐκέρδησα ἐκέρδανα	κεκέρδαγκα κεκέρδακα	κεκέρδημαι	
κηρύσσω proclaim	κηρύξω	ἐκήρυξα	κεκήρυχα	κεκήρυγμαι	ἐκηρύχθην
κινέω move	κινήσω	ἐκίνησα			ἐκινήθην
κλαίω weep	κλαύσω	ἔκλαυσα		κέκλαυμαι κέκλαυσμαι	ἐκλαύσθην
κλάω break	κλάσω	ἔκλασα		κέκλασμαι	ἐκλάσθην
κλείω shut, lock	κλείσω	ἔκλεισα	κέκλεικα	κέκλεισμαι	ἐκλείσθην
κλέπτω steal	κλέψω	ἔκλεψα	κέκλοφα	κέκλεμμαι	ἐκλάπην ἐκλέφθην
κληρονομέω inherit, obtain	κληρονομήσω	ἐκληρονόμησα	κεκληρονόμηκα		

Present	Future	Aorist	Perfect Active	Perfect M/P	Aorist Passive
κλίνω — incline [trans.], decline [intrans.]	κλινῶ	ἔκλινα	κέκλικα	κέκλιμαι	ἐκλίθην
κοιμάω — sleep	κοιμήσω	ἐκοίμισα		κεκοίμημαι	ἐκοιμήθην
κοινόω — make common	κοινόσω	ἐκοίνωσα	κεκοίνωκα	κεκοίνωμαι	ἐκοινώθην
κοινωνέω — share	κοινωνήσω	ἐκοινώνησα	κεκοινώνηκα	κεκοινώνημαι	
κολάζω — punish	κολάσω	ἐκολασάμην		κεκόλασμαι	ἐκολάσθην
κομίζω — get	κομιῶ / κομίσω / κομιοῦμαι	ἐκόμισα	κεκόμικα	κεκόμισμαι	ἐκομίσθην
κοπιάω — become tired from struggle	κοπιάσω	ἐκοπίασα	κεκοπίακα		
κόπτω — cut off, beat the breast in mourning	κόψω	ἔκοψα	κέκοφα	κέκομμαι	ἐκόπην
κοσμέω — put in order, adorn		ἐκόσμησα		κεκόσμημαι	
κράζω — call out, scream	κράζω	ἔκραξα / ἐκέκραξα / ἔκραγον / ἐκέκραγον	κέκραγα		

κρατέω take hold of	κρατήσω	ἐκράτησα	κεκράτηκα	κεκράτημαι	
κραυγάζω utter a loud sound	κραυγάσω	ἐκραύγασα			
κρεμάννυμι	κρεμάσω	ἐκρέμασα	κεκρέμακα		ἐκρεμάσθην
κρεμάω					
κρεμάννύω					
κρεμάζω hang					
κρίνω judge	κρινῶ	ἔκρινα	κέκρικα	κέκριμαι	ἐκρίθην
κρύπτω	κρύψω	ἔκρυψα	κέκρυφα	κέκρυμμαι	ἐκρύφθην
-κρύβω conceal					ἐκύβην
κτάομαι procure, acquire	κτήσομαι	ἐκτησάμην		κέκτημαι	
κτίζω create	κτίσω	ἔκτισα	ἔκτικα	ἔκτισμαι	ἐκτίσθην
κυριεύω control	κυριεύσω	ἐκυρίευσα			
κωλύω hinder, prevent, forbid	κωλύσω	ἐκώλυσα	κεκώλυκα	κεκώλυμαι	ἐκωλύθην
λαγχάνω be chosen by lot	λήξομαι	ἔλαχον	εἴληχα	εἴληγμαι	ἐλήχθην
λάζομαι	λάζομαι				

λαλέω speak	λαλήσω	ἐλάλησα	λελάληκα	λελάλημαι	ἐλαλήθην
λαμβάνω take, receive	λήμψομαι	ἔλαβον	εἴληφα λελάβηκα	εἴλημμαι	ἐλήφθην ἐλήμφθην
λάμπω shine	λάμψω	ἔλαμψα	λέλαμπα.		ἐλάμφθην
λανθάνω λήθω be hidden, escape notice	λήσω	ἔλαθον ἔλησα	λέληθα	λέλησμαι λέλασμαι	ἐλήσθην
λατρεύω serve = worship	λατρεύσω	ἐλάτρευσα			
λέγω say	ἐρῶ	εἶπον εἶπα	εἴρηκα	εἴρημαι	ἐρρέθην
λείπω lack, leave	λείψω	ἔλιπον ἔλειψα	λέλοιπα	λέλειμμαι	ἐλείφθην
λειτουργέω λῃτουργέω serve publicly	λειτουργήσω	ἐλειτούργησα	λελειτούργηκα		
λιθάζω stone		ἐλίθασα			ἐλιθάσθην
λογίζομαι consider	λογιοῦμαι	ἐλογισάμην		λελόγισμαι	ἐλογίσθην
λοιδορέω revile, reproach	λοιδορήσω	ἐλοιδόρησα	λελοιδόρηκα		

Present	Future	Aorist	Perfect Active	Perfect Mid/Pass	Aorist Passive
λούω — wash, bathe	λούσω / λοῦσω	ἔλουσα		λέλουμαι	ἐλούθην
λυπέω — grieve, pain		ἐλύπησα	λελύπηκα		ἐλυπήθην
λυτρόομαι — redeem		ἐλυτρωσάμην		λελύτρωμαι	ἐλυτρώθην
μαθητεύω — be or make a disciple, teach		ἐμαθήτευσα		μεμαθήτευμαι	ἐμαθητεύθην
μαίνομαι — act crazy	μανοῦμαι				ἐμάνην
μανθάνω — learn	μαθήσομαι	ἔμαθον	μεμάθηκα		
μαρτυρέω — testify as a witness	μαρτυρήσω	ἐμαρτύρησα	μεμαρτύρηκα	μεμαρτύρημαι	ἐμαρτυρήθην
μαστιγόω — whip	μαστιγώσω	ἐμαστίγωσα		μεμαστίγωμαι	ἐμαστιγώθην
μάχομαι — fight	μαχοῦμαι / μαχέσομαι	ἐμαχεσάμην			ἐμαχέσθην
μεγαλύνω — magnify	μεγαλυνῶ	ἐμεγάλυνα		μεμεγάλυσμαι	ἐμεγαλύνθην
μεθύσκω — become intoxicated	μεθύσω	ἐμέθυσα			ἐμεθύσθην
μέλλω — to be destined or about to be	μελλήσω	ἐμέλλησα / ἤμελλησα			

		Future	Aorist	Perfect	Perfect M/P	Aorist Passive
μένω	remain	μενῶ	ἔμεινα	μεμένηκα		
μερίζω	divide, distribute	μεριῶ	ἐμέρισα	μεμέρικα	μεμέρισμαι	ἐμερίσθην
μεριμνάω	be concerned about	μεριμνήσω	ἐμερίμνησα			
μεταβαίνω	move	μεταβήσομαι	μετέβην	μεταβέβηκα		
μεταλαμβάνω	receive one's share	μεταλήψομαι	μετέλαβον	μετείληφα	μετείλημμαι	
μετανοέω	repent	μετανοήσω	μετενόησα			
μετατίθημι	change	μεταθήσω	μετέθηκα	μετατέθεικα		μετετέθην
μετέχω	participate, share	μεθέξω	μετέσχον	μετέσχηκα		
μηνύω	inform	μηνύσω	ἐμήνυσα	μεμήνυκα	μεμήνυμαι	
μιαίνω	stain	μιανῶ	ἐμίανα / ἔμηνα	μεμίαγκα	μεμίαμμαι	ἐμιάνθην
μιμνῄσκομαι	remember	μνησθήσομαι / μνήσομαι			μέμνημαι	ἐμνήσθην
μισέω	hate	μισήσω	ἐμίσησα	μεμίσηκα	μεμίσημαι	ἐμισήθην

Present	Future	Aorist	Perfect Active	Perfect M/P	Aorist Passive
μνημονεύω remember, mention	μνημονεύσω	ἐμνημόνευσα	μεμνημόνευκα	μεμνημόνευμαι	ἐμνημονεύθην
μοιχεύω commit adultery	μοιχεύσω	ἐμοίχευσα			
μολύνω make impure, stain	μολυνῶ	ἐμόλυνα	μεμόλυγκα	μεμόλυμμαι	ἐμολύνθην
μωραίνω become foolish, tasteless	μωρανῶ	ἐμώρανα			ἐμωράνθην
νηστεύω fast	νηστεύσω	ἐνήστευσα			
νικάω overcome	νικήσω	ἐνίκησα	νενίκηκα		
νίπτω = νίζω wash	νίψω	ἔνιψα		νένιμμαι	ἐνίφθην
νοέω understand	νοήσω	ἐνόησα	νενόηκα	νενόημαι	ἐνοήθην
νομίζω be the custom, consider	νομίσω	ἐνόμισα		νενόμισμαι	ἐνομίσθην
νομοθετέω legislate, ordain	νομοθετήσω	ἐνομοθέτησα	νενομοθέτηκα	νενομοθέτημαι	
νουθετέω warn	νουθετήσω	ἐνουθέτησα			

ξενίζω entertain, surprise	ξενίσω	ἐξένισα			ἐξενίσθην
ξηραίνω dry up	ξηρανῶ	ἐξήρανα		ἐξήραμμαι ἐξήρασμαι	ἐξηράνθην
οἶδα=2 Perf. of [εἴδω] know	εἰδήσω εἴσομαι		οἶδα ᾔδειν 2 Pluperf.		
(see', used only in 2 aor. εἴδον; ὁράω replaces εἴδω in pres.)					
οἰκέω dwell	οἰκήσω	ᾤκησα	ᾤκηκα	ᾤκημαι	ᾠκήθην
οἰκοδομέω build	οἰκοδομήσω	ᾠκοδόμησα	ᾠκοδόμηκα		ᾠκοδομήθην οἰκοδομήθην
ὀμνύω ὄμνυμι take an oath, swear	ὀμοῦμαι ὀμόσω	ὤμοσα	ὀμώμοκα	ὀμώμοται (3 s.)	ὠμόθην ὠμόσθην
ὁμοιόω resemble, compare	ὁμοιώσω	ὡμοίωσα		ὡμοίωμαι	ὡμοιώθην
ὁμολογέω confess	ὁμολογήσω	ὡμολόγησα	ὡμολόγηκα	ὡμολόγημαι	ὡμολογήθην
ὀνειδίζω reproach	ὀνειδιῶ	ὠνείδισα	ὠνείδικα		ὠνειδίσθην
ὀνομάζω name	ὀνομάσω	ὠνόμασα	ὠνόμακα	ὠνόμασμαι	ὠνομάσθην
ὁράω see	ὄψομαι	[εἴδον]	ἑώρακα	ἑώραμαι	ὤφθην ἑωράθην

182

ὀργίζομαι be angry	ὀργιοῦμαι	ὤργισα		ὤργισμαι	ὠργίσθην
ὁρίζω determine, set	ὁριῶ	ὥρισα	ὤρικα	ὥρισμαι	ὡρίσθην
ὁρμάω rush	ὁρμήσω	ὥρμησα	ὥρμηκα	ὥρμημαι	ὡρμήθην
ὀρύσσω dig	ὀρύξω	ὤρυξα	ὀρόρυχα	ὀρώρυγμαι ὤρυγμαι	ὠρύχθην ὠρύγην
ὀφείλω owe	ὀφειλήσω	ὠφείλησα ὤφελον	ὠφείληκα		
παιδεύω educate	παιδεύσω	ἐπαίδευσα	πεπαίδευκα	πεπαίδευμαι	ἐπαιδεύθην
παίω hit	παίσω παιήσω	ἔπαισα	πέπαικα	πέπαισμαι	ἐπαίσθην
παλαιόω become old	παλαιώσω	ἐπαλαίωσα	πεπαλαίωκα		ἐπαλαιώθην
παραγγέλλω give orders, direct	παραγγελῶ	παρήγγειλα			
παραγίνομαι be present		παρεγενόμην			παρεγενήθην
παραδίδωμι hand over	παραδώσω	παρέδωκα	παραδέδωκα		παρεδόθην

παρακαλέω invite, encourage	παρακαλῶ παρακαλέσω	παρεκάλεσα		παρεκέκλημαι	παρεκλήθην
παρακολουθέω follow	παρακολουθήσω	παρηκολούθησα	παρηκολούθηκα		
παρατίθημι place beside	παραθήσω	παρέθηκα παρεθέμην	παρατέθεικα		παρετέθην
παρέρχομαι pass	παρελεύσομαι	παρῆλθον	παρελήλυθα		
παρέχω grant, show	παρέξω	παρέσχον	παρέσχηκα		
παρίστημι παριστάνω present	παραστήσω	παρέστησα παρέστην	παρέστηκα		παρεστάθην
παρρησιάζομαι speak freely	παρρησιάσομαι	ἐπαρρησιασάμην			
πάσχω suffer	πείσομαι	ἔπαθον	πέπονθα πέποσχα		
πατάσσω hit, strike	πατάξω	ἐπάταξα		πεπάταγμαι	ἐπατάχθην
πατέω tread on, trample	πατήσω				ἐπατήθην
παύω cease, stop	παύσω	ἔπαυσα	πέπαυκα	πέπαυμαι	ἐπαύθην ἐπαύσθην ἐπάην

πείθω persuade	πείσω	ἔπεισα	πέποιθα	πέπεισμαι	ἐπείσθην
πεινάω hunger	πεινάσω	ἐπείνασα	πεπείνηκα		
πειράζω try, trust	πειράσω πειράξω	ἐπείρασα		πεπείρασμαι	ἐπειράσθην
πέμπω send	πέμψω	ἔπεμψα	πέπομφα		ἐπέμφθην
πενθέω grieve	πενθήσω	ἐπένθησα	πεπένθηκα		
περιβάλλω put around	περιβαλῶ	περιέβαλον			
περιζώννυμι περιζωννύω bind something around oneself	περιζώσομαι	περιεζωσάμην			
περιπατέω walk around	περιπατήσω	περιεπάτησα			
περισσεύω abound	περισσεύσω	ἐπερίσσευσα			
περιτέμνω circumcise		περιέτεμον			περιετμήθην
πήγνυμι put together firmly	πήξω	ἔπηξα	πέπηγα	πέπηγμαι	ἐπήχθην ἐπάγην

πιάζω grasp, arrest		ἐπίασα			ἐπιάσθην
πίμπλημι fill, fulfill	πλήσω	ἔπλησα	πέπληκα	πέπλησμαι	ἐπλήσθην
πίνω drink	πίομαι πιοῦμαι	ἔπιον	πέπωκα		ἐπόθην
πιπράσκω sell			πέπρακα		ἐπράθην
πίπτω fall	πεσοῦμαι	ἔπεσον ἔπεσα	πέπτωκα		
πιστεύω believe	πιστεύσω	ἐπίστευσα	πεπίστευκα	πεπίστευμαι	ἐπιστεύθην
πλανάω wander away	πλανήσω	ἐπλάνησα		πεπλάνημαι	ἐπλανήθην
πλάσσω form, mold	πλάσω	ἔπλασα	πέπλακα	πέπλασμαι	ἐπλάσθην
πλεονάζω increase	πλεονάσω	ἐπλεόνασα	πεπλεόνακα	πεπλεόνασμαι	ἐπλεονάσθην
πλεονεκτέω outwit, cheat	πλεονεκτήσω	ἐπλεονέκτησα			ἐπλεονεκτήθην
πλέω sail	πλεύσομαι πλευσοῦμαι	ἔπλευσα	πέπλευκα	πέπλευσμαι	ἐπλεύσθην

	Future	Aorist	Perfect Active	Perfect M/P	Aorist Passive
πληθύνω increase	πληθυνῶ	ἐπλήθυνα			ἐπληθύνθην
πληροφορέω fill out, convince		ἐπληροφόρησα		πεπληροφόρημαι	
πληρόω fill, fulfill, finish	πληρώσω	ἐπλήρωσα	πεπλήρωκα	πεπλήρωμαι	ἐπληρώθην
πλήσσω strike	πλήξω	ἔπληξα	πέπληγα πέπληχα		ἐπλήχθην ἐπλήγην
πλουτέω be rich		ἐπλούτησα	πεπλούτηκα		
πλουτίζω make rich	πλουτιῶ	ἐπλούτισα			ἐπλουτίσθην
πνέω blow	πνεύσω πνευσοῦμαι	ἔπνευσα	πέπνευκα		ἐπνεύσθην
ποιέω make, do	ποιήσω	ἐποίησα	πεποίηκα	πεποίημαι	ἐποιήθην
ποιμαίνω herd, tend	ποιμανῶ	ἐποίμανα			
πολεμέω fight	πολεμήσω	ἐπολέμησα	πεπολέμηκα	πεπολέμημαι	ἐπολεμήθην
πολιτεύομαι live one's life		ἐπολιτευσάμην		πεπολίτευμαι	

Present	Future	Aorist	Perfect Active	Perfect M/P	Aorist Passive
πορεύομαι proceed, travel	πορεύσομαι	ἐπόρευσα		πεπόρευμαι	ἐπορεύθην
ποτίζω give a drink, water	ποτιῶ	ἐπότισα	πεπότικα		ἐποτίσθην
πράσσω accomplish, do	πράξω	ἔπραξα	πέπραχα	πέπραγμαι	ἐπράχθην
πρέπω be proper, suitable	πρέψω	ἔπρεψα			
προάγω lead the way	προάξω	προήγαγον	προῆχα		
προαιρέω choose, prefer	προαιρήσω	προεῖλον		προῄρημαι	
προγράφω write beforehand, portray publicly	προγράφω	προέγραψα			προεγράφην
[προεῖπον] mention before, foretell	προερῶ	προεῖπον	προείρηκα		
προέρχομαι go (forward, before, out)	προελεύσομαι	προῆλθον	προελήλυθα		
προΐστημι manage, care for	προϊστήσω	προΰστησα			
προσδέχομαι welcome, wait for		προσεδεξάμην			προσεδέχθην

Present	Future	Aorist	Perfect Active	Perfect Mid/Pass	Aorist Passive
προσέρχομαι go to, approach	προσελύσομαι	προσῆλθον	προσελήλυθα		
προσεύχομαι pray	προσεύξομαι	προσηυξάμην			
προσέχω pay attention to		προσέσχον	προσέσχηκα		
προσκαλέω summon		προσεκαλεσάμην		προσκέκλημαι	
προσκυνέω do obeisance to	προσκυνήσω	προσεκύνησα	προσκεκύνηκα		προσεκυνήθην
προσλαμβάνω take (aside, along), accept		προσέλαβον	προσείληφα		
προσπίπτω fall down, strike against	προσπεσοῦμαι	προσέπεσον / προσέπεσα			
προστίθημι add	προσθήσω	προσέθηκα / προσεθέμην		προστέθειμαι	προσετέθην
προσφέρω bring, offer	προσοίσω	προσήνεγκον / προσηνεγκα / προσένεικα	προσενήνοχα		προσηνέχθην / προσηνείχθην
προφητεύω prophesy	προφητεύσω	ἐπροφήτευσα			
πταίω stumble	πταίσω	ἔπταισα	ἔπταικα		

πυνθάνομαι inquire, investigate	πεύσομαι	ἐπυθόμην		πέπυσμαι	
πωλέω sell	πωλήσω	ἐπώλησα			ἐπωλήθην
πωρόω petrify	πωρώσω	ἐπώρωσα	πεπώρωκα		ἐπωρώθην
ῥαντίζω sprinkle, purify	ῥαντιῶ	ἐράντισα			
ῥήγνυμι ῥήσσω tear, burst, break out	ῥήξω	ἔρρηξα	ἔρρηχα	ἔρρηγμαι	ἐρρήχθην
ῥίπτω ῥιπτέω throw	ῥίψω	ἔρριψα	ἔρριφα	ἔρριμμαι	ἐρρίφθην ἐρρίφην
ῥύομαι rescue, deliver	ῥύσομαι	ἐρρυσάμην			ἐρρύσθην
σαλεύω shake	σαλεύσω	ἐσάλευσα		σεσάλευμαι	ἐσαλεύθην
σαλπίζω trumpet	σαλπίσω σαλπιῶ	ἐσάλπισα ἐσάλπιγξα		σεσάλπιγκται (3 s.)	
σβέννυμι extinguish	σβέσω	ἔσβεσα	ἔσβηκα	ἔσβεσμαι	ἐσβέσθην

Present	Future	Aorist	Perfect	Perfect M/P	Aorist Passive
σείω shake	σείσω	ἔσεισα	σέσεικα	σέσεισμαι	ἐσείσθην
σημαίνω indicate beforehand, signify	σημανῶ	ἐσήμηνα ἐσήμανα	σεσήμαγκα	σεσήμασμαι	ἐσημάνθην
σιγάω be silent	σιγήσω	ἐσίγησα	σεσίγηκα	σεσίγημαι	ἐσιγήθην
σιωπάω be silent	σιωπήσω	ἐσιώπησα	σεσιώπηκα		
σκανδαλίζω cause to stumble		ἐσκανδάλισα			ἐσκανδαλίσθην
σκηνόω pitch tents, dwell	σκηνόωσω	ἐσκήνωσα			
σκληρύνω harden	σκληρύνω	ἐσκλήρυνα		ἐσκλήρυσμαι	ἐσκληρύνθην
σκοπέω notice	σκοπήσω	ἐσκόπησα		ἐσκόπημαι	
σκορπίζω scatter	σκορπιῶ	ἐσκόρπισα			ἐσκορπίσθην
σκοτίζομαι become dark				ἐσκότισμαι	ἐσκοτίσθην
σπείρω sow	σπερῶ	ἔσπειρα	ἔσπαρκα	ἔσπαρμαι	ἐσπάρην

σπεύδω hurry	σπεύσω	ἔσπευσα	ἔσπευκα	ἔσπευσμαι	
σπουδάζω be eager	σπουδάσω	ἐσπούδασα	ἐσπούδακα	ἐσπούδασμαι	ἐσπουδάσθην
σταυρόω crucify	σταυρόσω	ἐσταύρωσα		ἐσταύρωμαι	ἐσταυρώθην
στενάζω sigh, groan	στενάξω	ἐστέναξα		ἐστέναγμαι	
στηρίζω establish	στηρίζω στηριῶ	ἐστήριξα ἐστήρισα		ἐστήριγμαι	ἐστηρίχθην
στρέφω turn	στρέψω	ἔστρεψα	ἔστροφα ἔστραφα ἔστροκα	ἔστραμμαι	ἐστράφην ἐστρέφθην ἐστρώθην
στρωννύω στρώννυμι στόρνυμι spread out	στορῶ στρόσω	ἐστόρεσα		ἐστόρεσμαι	
συγχέω συγχύννω [pour together], confuse, trouble		συνέχεα		συγκέχυμαι	συνεχύθην
συλλαμβάνω grasp, support	συλλήμψομαι	συνέλαβον	συνείληφα	συνείλημμαι	συνελήμφθην
συμβαίνω meet, happen	συμβήσομαι	συνέβην	συμβέβηκα		

Present	Future	Aorist	Perfect	Perfect M/P	Aorist Passive
συμβιβάζω	συμβιβάσω	συνεβίβασα			
συμφέρω		συνήνεγκα / συνήνεγκον	συνενήνοχα		
συμφωνέω	συμφωνήσω	συνεφώνησα			
συνάγω	συνάξω	συνήγαγον / συνῆξα	συνῆχα	συνῆγμαι	συνήχθην
συνεργέω		συνήργησα	συνήργηκα		
συνέρχομαι	συνελεύσομαι	συνῆλθον	συνελήλυθα		
συνέχω	συνέξω	συνέσχον			
συνίημι / συνίω	συνήσω	συνῆκα	συνεῖκα		
συνίστημι / συνιστάνω / συνιστάω	συστήσω	συνέστησα	συνέστηκα / συνέστακα		
συντελέω	συντελέσω				συντελέσθην

συμβιβάζω — bring together, conclude, prove, teach [causal form of συμβαίνω]

συμφέρω — be beneficial

συμφωνέω — agree, harmonize

συνάγω — gather

συνεργέω — work with, cooperate

συνέρχομαι — assemble, travel together

συνέχω — hold together, press hard

συνίημι, συνίω — understand

συνίστημι, συνιστάνω, συνιστάω — present, demonstrate, commend, continue

συντελέω — complete, accomplish

Present	Future	Aorist	Perfect Active	Perfect M/P	Aorist Passive
συντρέχω run together	συνδραμοῦμαι	συνέδραμον	συνδεδράμηκα		
συντρίβω smash, crush	συντρίψω	συνέτριψα			συνετρίβην
σφάζω σφάττω slaughter	σφάξω	ἔσφαξα	ἔσφακα	ἔσφαγμαι	ἐσφάγην ἐσφάχθην
σφραγίζω seal		ἐσφράγισα			ἐσφραγίσθην
σχίζω split	σχίσω	ἔσχισα		ἔσχισμαι	ἐσχίσθην
σῴζω save	σώσω	ἔσωσα	σέσωκα	σέσωσμαι σέσωμαι	ἐσώθην
ταπεινόω make low	ταπεινώσω	ἐταπείνωσα			ἐταπεινώθην
ταράσσω stir up	ταράξω	ἐτάραξα	τέτρηκα	τετάραγμαι	ἐταράχθην
τάσσω place, appoint, determine	τάξω	ἔταξα	τέταχα	τέταγμαι	ἐτάχθην ἐτάγην
τελειόω complete		ἐτελείωσα	τετελείοκα	τετελείωμαι	ἐτελειώθην
τελευτάω come to an end, die	τελευτήσω	ἐτελεύτησα	τετελεύτηκα		ἐτελευτήθην

	Future	Aorist	Perfect Active	Perfect Mid./Pass.	Aorist Passive
τελέω finish	τελέσω	ἐτέλεσα	τετέλεκα	τετέλεσμαι	ἐτελέσθην
τηρέω keep, guard, preserve	τηρήσω	ἐτήρησα	τετήρηκα	τετήρημαι	ἐτηρήθην
τίθημι τιθέω put, place	θήσω	ἔθηκα ἐθέμην ἔθην	τέθεικα τέθηκα	τέθειμαι	ἐτέθην
τίκτω give birth to	τέξω	ἔτεκον ἐτεξα	τέτοκα	τέτεγμαι	ἐτέχθην
τιμάω value, honor	τιμήσω	ἐτίμησα	τετίμηκα	τετίμημαι	ἐτιμήθην
τολμάω dare	τολμήσω	ἐτόλμησα	τετόλμηκα		
τρέφω feed	θρέψω	ἔθρεψα	τέτροφα τέτραφα	τέθραμμαι	ἐθρέφθην ἐτράφην
τρέχω θρέξομαι δραμοῦμαι run	θρέξομαι δραμοῦμαι	ἔδραμον ἔθρεξα	δεδράμηκα	δεδράμημαι	
τυγχάνω meet, experience, happen to be	τεύξομαι	ἔτυχον ἐτύχησα	τέτευχα τετύχηκα	τέτευγμαι	ἐτεύχθην
τύπτω strike, beat	τύψω τυπτήσω	ἔτυψα ἐτύπτησα ἔτυπον	τέτυφα τετύπτηκα	τέτυμμαι τετύπτημαι	ἐτύφθην ἐτυπτήθην ἐτύπην

[cf. πατάσσω 'strike', used in the fut. and aor. in Attic & LXX.]

τυφλόω blind		ἐτύφλωσα	τετύφλωκα		
ὑβρίζω mistreat	ὑβριῶ	ὕβρισα	ὕβρικα	ὕβρισμαι	ὑβρίσθην
ὑγιαίνω be healthy	ὑγιανῶ	ὑγίανα			
ὑμνέω sing praise	ὑμνήσω	ὕμνησα			
ὑπακούω obey, grant one's request	ὑπακούσομαι	ὑπήκουσα			
ὑπάρχω exist, be present, be	ὑπάρξω	ὑπῆρξα		ὑπῆργμαι	
ὑπερέχω have power over, surpass	ὑπερέξω	ὑπερέσχον			
ὑποδείκνυμι, ὑποδεικνύω show, indicate	ὑποδείξω	ὑπέδειξα			
ὑπομένω remain	ὑπομενῶ	ὑπέμεινα			
ὑπομιμνῄσκω remind	ὑπομνήσω	ὑπέμνησα			ὑπεμνήσθην
ὑποτάσσω subject, be subordinated	ὑποταγήσομαι	ὑπέταξα		ὑποτέταγμαι	ὑπετάγην

Present	Future	Aorist	Perfect Active	Perfect Mid./Pass.	Aorist Passive
ὑστερέω — miss, lack, be inferior	ὑστερήσω	ὑστέρησα	ὑστέρηκα		ὑστερήθην
ὑψόω — lift up	ὑψώσω	ὕψωσα			ὑψώθην
φαίνω — shine	φανῶ	ἔφανα	πέφαγκα	πέφασμαι	ἐφάνην
	φανήσομαι	ἔφηνα	πέφηνα		ἐφάνθην
φανερόω — reveal	φανερώσω	ἐφανέρωσα	πεφανέρωκα	πεφανέρομαι	ἐφανερώθην
φείδομαι — spare, refrain	φείσομαι	ἐφεισάμην			
φέρω — bear, carry	οἴσω	ἤνεγκα / ἤνεγκον	ἐνήνοχα	ἐνήνεγμαι	ἠνέχθην
φεύγω — flee, escape	φεύξομαι	ἔφυγον	πέφευγα		
φημί — say	φήσω	ἔφην / ἔφη / ἔφησα			ἐφάθην
φθάνω — precede, arrive	φθήσομαι	ἔφθασα	ἔφθακα / πέφθακα		ἐφθάσθην
φθείρω — destroy, corrupt	φθερῶ	ἔφθειρα	ἔφθαρκα	ἔφθαρμαι	ἐφθάρην
φιλέω — love	φιλήσω	ἐφίλησα	πεφίληκα	πεφίλημαι	ἐφιλήθην

φιμόω tie shut, muzzle	φιμώσω	ἐφίμωσα			
φοβέω be afraid	φοβήσω	ἐφόβησα		πεφόβημαι	ἐφοβήθην
φονεύω murder	φονεύσω	ἐφόνευσα			
φορέω wear	φορέσω	ἐφόρεσα	πεφόρηκα	πεφόρημαι	ἐφορήθην
	φορήσω	ἐφόρησα			
φρονέω think	φρονήσω	ἐφρόνησα	πεφρόνηκα		
φρουρέω confine, guard	φρουρήσω	ἐφρούρησα		πεφρούρημαι	ἐφρουρήθην
φυλάσσω protect	φυλάξω	ἐφύλαξα	πεφύλαχα	πεφύλαγμαι	ἐφυλάχθην
φυτεύω plant	φυτεύσω	ἐφύτευσα	πεφύτευκα	πεφύτευμαι	ἐφυτεύθην
φύω grow up	φύσω	ἔφυσα	πέφυκα		ἐφύην
	φυήσω				
φωνέω call	φωνήσω	ἐφώνησα			ἐφωνήθην
φωτίζω give light	φωτίσω	ἐφώτισα			ἐφωτίσθην
	φωτῶ				

Present	Future	Aorist	Perfect Active	Perfect Mid./Pass.	Aorist Passive
χαίρω rejoice	χαρήσομαι	ἐχαίρησα	κεχάρηκα	κεχάρημαι	ἐχάρην
χαλάω let down, lower	χαλάσω	ἐχάλασα		κεχάλασμαι	ἐχαλάσθην
χαρίζομαι give freely, forgive	χαρίσομαι	ἐχαρισάμην		κεχάρισμαι	ἐχαρίσθην
χορτάζω feed, satisfy	χορτάσω	ἐχόρτασα			ἐχορτάσθην
χράομαι use	χρήσομαι	ἐχρησάμην		κέχρημαι	ἐχρήσθην
χρηματίζω give a revelation or warning, be called or named	χρηματίσω	ἐχρημάτισα	κεχρημάτικα	κεχρημάτισμαι	ἐχρηματίσθην
χρίω anoint	χρίσω	ἔχρισα	κέχρικα	κέχριμαι κέχρισμαι	ἐχρίσθην
χωρέω make room, give way	χωρήσω	ἐχώρησα	κεχώρηκα	κεχώρηται (3 s.)	ἐχωρήθην
χωρίζω divide	χωρίσω	ἐχώρισα		κεχώρισμαι	ἐχωρίσθην
ψάλλω sing	ψαλῶ	ἔψηλα ἔψαλα			
ψεύδομαι lie	ψεύσομαι	ἐψευσάμην		ἔψευσμαι	

ψηλαφάω	ψηλαφήσω	ἐψηλάφησα			ἐψηλαφήθην
feel, grope after					
ὠδίνω	ὠδινήσω	ὤδινα			
suffer birth pains		ὠδίνησα			
ὠφελέω	ὠφελήσω	ὠφέλησα	ὠφέληκα	ὠφέλημαι	ὠφελήθην
help, benefit, be used to					

All verb entries are based on either Bauer-Arndt-Gingrich-Danker, *Greek-English Lexicon of the NT and Other Early Christian Literature*, second edition, University of Chicago Press, 1979, or on Liddell and Scott, *Greek-English Lexicon*, Oxford at the Clarendon Press, ninth edition, reprinted in 1978.

The *Principles of Inclusion* in the Verb Bank are as follows: All verbs occurring seven times or more combined in the LXX and NT that have at least two principal parts beyond the lexical form (the present tense) appear in the Verb Bank. A few are included that have less than seven occurrences. Verbs like γέμω ('be full'), κεῖμαι ('lie down') and στήκω ('stand') are not included because they occur only in the present and imperfect built on the present stem. The bank is *intended to provide principal parts for parsing purposes.*

Analytical lexicons are useful occasionally for parsing a difficult verb form. However, the preferred way to recognize correct parsing is achieved by using a verb bank for principal parts, and (if need be) a λύω chart for prefixes and suffixes: (See pages 11–17; 21–26; 28–29; 33–34; 37–39; 54; 61–62.) The Verb Bank enables the eye, revealing all a verb's principal parts in configuration, and in a visual context of other alphabetically similar spellings. Because of the superiority of visual memory (over an answer book), the more the Verb Bank is used early on, the less it will be needed later on. Not so with analytical lexicons.

INDEX OF BIBLICAL CITATIONS

John (cont.)

Ref	Page	Ref	Page	Ref	Page
5:45	50	8:12	119	12:27	46
6:6	143	8:31	41	12:29	53
6:10	92	8:32	32	12:32	45
6:17	8	8:38	102	12:33	32
6:21	53	8:39	127	12:47	81
6:27	50, 58	8:40	102	13:13	77
6:35	46	8:42	28	13:19	51
6:37	55	9:2	44	13:36	43
6:40	42	9:5	119	14:7	43
6:50	121	10:3	116	14:11	6
6:57	58	10:11	116	14:26	89
6:62	91	10:24	127	14:27	122
6:63	55	10:31	44	15:19	128
6:65	36	10:37	127	15:22	128
6:69	36	11:2	149	15:26	4
7:4	127	11:8	146	16:2	52
7:23	127	11:19	150	16:23	123
7:30	120	11:22	45	18:30	124, 128
7:32	115	11:33	55	19:4–5	20
7:37	129	12:10	105	19:26	121
7:44	115	12:12	145	19:40	52
7:45	115	12:18	90	20:15	127
8:9	78	12:20	136	20:17	135
		12:22	20	20:20	56

INDEX OF KEY TERMS AND PARADIGMS

Note: All the verbal paradigms have been set up in the order of Tense, Mood, Voice.